Reflections on Luther's Catechism

# this
# FAitH
## is
# MiNe

**By R. Z. Meyer**

NCORDIA PUBLISHING HOUSE • SAINT LOUIS

# This book
# is a gift to

---

*For the eyes of the Lord are on the righteous*
*and His ears are attentive to their prayer. I Peter 3:12*

From:

Date:

# Contents

# Introduction

As Lutheran youth most of you are well acquainted with Dr. Martin Luther's Small Catechism. It, along with the Bible, has been the basic text for your public confirmation of the Christian faith. Most of you have memorized these chief parts of the faith and, as a result, they have become the way you think and express your understanding of the truths in God's Word.

The reflections in this book have been based on the Small Catechism. The purpose has been to remind you what you have been taught and at the same time to make every part of the faith relevant and vital to your daily life. Since the source of all teaching in the Lutheran church is the Bible, each reflection has one to three short studies in the Holy Scriptures. These studies develop the thought of the reflection, leading you into the Word itself. It is in the Word of God that true and lasting growth comes.

This book is designed to be a private devotional for your life. The reflections have not been designed for rapid reading. Allow yourself plenty of time. First read the devotional thoughts on one of the chief parts of the faith, then open up your Bible and study the thoughts of the reflection. Since it is only in the atmosphere of prayer that any fruitful growth can come, each reflection should be begun in the holy name of the Triune God and ended in serious and thought-filled prayer.

Reflections on

# The Apostles' Creed

## "I believe..."

You begin the Christian church's well-known Apostles' Creed with the little word "I." With this short but all-important word you are all alone.

There are times when we should use the word "we." Look back across the centuries and see the countless number of saints, apostles, and martyrs—people no different than you—who have confessed this very creed. Look about you across nations and peoples and see millions who stand up for Jesus. Look into the future and see "ten thousand times ten thousand" and thousands of thousands who will be praising the triune God. It is a thrilling thought to be included among such a multitude of men and women. Each one of them had to begin like you—all alone—with the little word "I." There is no other way around it.

To begin with the word "I" may be a very disturbing thing, because it leaves you all alone—all alone with God—all alone with the world. At first you may not like it at all. You are naturally a social person; you like to be with people. You like to be doing what the next person is doing. You want to know what the popular clothing styles are. You like to know what your friends are saying. Let's face it! Most of the time it is the kids at school or your friends that help you make your decisions. But now at the all-important moment in your life you are all alone, alone with your God and alone with yourself.

But this is the way God wants it. He wants you to face Him by yourself. He doesn't want you to run to anybody else. He doesn't want you to depend on anything other than Him. God wants you to be able to stand on your own two feet. He wants you to be so certain in the depths of your heart and so unafraid in the life of your own soul that He, and He alone, is the center of everything you think, say, or do. This is what God wants.

So you begin the creed, "*I believe.*" As every other man or woman of God, you begin the confession of your own faith. It isn't always comfortable and it can be very disturbing at times, but it is the beginning of an eternal life with God.

# Reflections

Read 1 Samuel 1:1 to 2:10. Hannah is hardly unfamiliar to you. Did you ever stop to think how lonely she must have been in her faith? Her husband loved her (1:8). Eli, who was her priest, comforted her (1:17). But she was forced to be alone with her God and herself (1:10–11). She had to take the leap of faith and trust solely in her God. She couldn't take her husband with her, nor could she take Eli, the priest. She had to do it alone. Hannah was learning the meaning of "*I believe.*" God can and does do wonders with people like her. Read over and over again her song of praise (2:1–10), and catch the thrill of her faith in such phrases as "My heart . . . my strength . . . my mouth . . . I rejoice." Hannah would share this joy of her faith with you. She wants God to be as big and as strong for you as He was for her. Every person who begins the creed, "*I believe,*" must be ready to take the leap of faith and confess on his or her own two feet the conviction within him or her.

Read Exodus 2:23 to 3:22. Compare this Old Testament account with the New Testament's interpretation in →

Hebrews 11:23–28. The courts of Egypt were hardly the popular place to confessing "I believe in God the Father Almighty." Moses was very much alone in his faith. He was threatened with many personal fears and doubts during those many years, such as the fear of public speaking (Exodus 4:10). Yet God can do big things with a person who will believe in Him and in Him alone. Moses believed his sufferings for the Christ were greater wealth than the treasures of Egypt. His strength, like his faith came solely from God.

You would think that Moses was now prepared to be the leader of God's people. God did not think so. The second phase of Moses' schooling was in the desert wastelands around Mount Sinai. Where Egypt was mankind's school, the desert was God's. It was here that Moses was alone with his God—alone in meditation and prayer—alone with his sheep. You see, Moses, like everybody else, had to begin in the faith with the little word "I." There is no other way. Actually you are always "beginning" in the Christian faith. You don't say on the day of your confirmation "*I* believe," and feel you have arrived. But when you say "*I* believe," you are certain that God will help you to arrive at real maturity—that measure of development which is meant by "the fullness of Christ." And you will become better and better prepared for the task God has chosen for you.

## "I believe ..."

The word "believe" may mean many things. When a child jumps unhesitatingly from a tree branch into his or her father's arms, you say that the child has faith in the father. When you are lost and are forced to ask a policeman the way, you happily follow his directions, trusting in his knowledge of the city. Yet there is more to the meaning of "believe." It can be far deeper and more intimate.

When a little child believes in a parent, this is more than just trust and knowledge. It means more than just knowing he or she exists or that Mom can fix all hurts or that Dad can fix any broken toy. It even means more than knowing they love you. For a little child to believe in a parent means to him or her, the parent's ideas are wonderful, and he or she wishes to be part of them. The child adores what the parent says and what he or she does.

Imagine a small child dressing up in the parent's clothes and acting like them. That child does so because he or she "worships the ground that Mom or Dad walks on." The little child happily does what Mom or Dad asks. The child is content to sit on his or her dad's lap and listen to him talk, just as Dad is happy to hear the child's stories. The child is certain that Dad can do anything. The child really believes in Dad!

This interaction between a child and parent is an example of the relationship that God wants between you and Himself. God wants you to believe in Him. He wants you to "worship the ground He walks on." He wants you to think that His ideas are wonderful, and He is happy when you want to become part of them. God delights in His children whenever they do little things just to please Him. He wants you to be happy and blessed because of your faith. This is what should take place between you and God when you say that you *believe.*

God knows that this is the only way that you will ever find yourself and be eternally happy. God knows far better than you that this is the only way you can discover what life is all about. And to those young men and women who understand the full meaning of believing in God the Father Almighty, He entrusts the stewardship of His kingdom. St. Paul had another way of saying "I believe." He confessed, "The life I now live in the body, I live by faith in the Son of God, who loved me and gave Himself for me" (Galatians 2:20). If this is your honest confession, you are beginning an adventurous life with God.

## Reflections

Read Genesis 12:1–9. For an explanation of this Old Testament record, see Hebrews 11:8–12. Faith results in motion. It never remains static. It always results in movement in God's direction. God said "Go!" and Abraham went. Abraham went solely upon God's word. He went out "not knowing where he was to go." His security rested in God and in Him alone. Little wonder that Abraham is called "the friend of God." Your faith is evident by its motion—motion that is moved by the Word of the Lord, even when your reason, your emotions, your friends cannot comprehend it. God wants to call you His friend. "Friend, are you ready for My directions?" You may not know what His directions will be. But you must be waiting on His Word. "Lord, I believe. . . . "

Read Genesis 6. Compare with Hebrews 11:6–7. Faith is conviction. To believe in God allows no compromise with anything that is not of God. God's grace was working in Noah. Every hammer blow foretold the coming judgment upon the wickedness of his generation. Every board put into place testified to people, "I believe in God the Father Almighty." So Noah became an "heir of the righteousness that comes by faith." As God looks upon our world today He must again be sad at mankind's sin. When God sees young men and women who believe in Him, He is overjoyed at those who do His will. God wants to look at you and see nothing soft or flighty, but a faith strong and solid. Faith is conviction—conviction that can spell out to our world God's grace and goodness, as well as His judgment and salvation.

Read 2 Kings 6:8–17. Faith is also vision. Haven't you found yourself saying in the words of the servant of Elisha, "What shall we do?" (2 Kings 6:15). The enemies of our faith seem so strong and overwhelming. We tremble as though God did not exist. True faith opens our eyes to see God in action. And God is bigger than all our enemies. When Jesus touches the eyes of a believer with His grace, he suddenly can see everything in life in its right perspective. God wants young people with vision, vision that can see God working mightily in this world—vision that can comprehend the height and width and depth of God's love (Romans 8:39), vision that permits you to act and speak boldly, knowing that terrorism has not lessened His power and that the media cannot outshine His love for the world. "Open my eyes that I may see" (Psalm 119:18).

## "I believe in God, the Father Almighty"

Every time you confess your faith in the Triune God, you remind yourself (as well as others) that a Christian approaches God with two basic attitudes—fear and love. The one is an attitude of reverence and awe; the other is an attitude of confidence and devotion.

You say, "I believe in God . . . Almighty." This is not to be said in a careless manner. Many young people have a very lighthearted attitude toward God. They think He is just the "friendly neighbor," the one who understands, the Guy who listens to all your troubles when you get a bit blue, the "Someone" out there. Much of contemporary American religious thinking places God and humanity on a "buddy-buddy" relationship. Little do such people realize the truth of the Scripture, "It is a dreadful, fearful thing to fall into the hands of the living God" (Hebrews 10:32).

You dare not treat God in a lighthearted manner. You may never approach God with an outstretched arm to pat Him on the back. Rather you should come to Him with outstretched hands asking for mercy. As Psalm 51:17 says, God will not despise "a broken and contrite heart," therefore your first attitude toward God the Almighty is one of reverence and awe.

But you also speak of God with confidence and devotion because you call Him "Father." To call God "Father" is a privilege given, not a right to be taken. God is everybody's God, but not everybody's Father. Many who claim Him as "Father" have no right to do so. They are not part of His family. They are illegitimate children, to say the least. But you can call God "Father" because He has adopted you into His heavenly family. If someone asks, "How do you know that you are adopted into God's family?" you answer, "God has adopted me because of His divine goodness. He has shown me His goodness in His Son. And because I know Jesus, I know the Father. But if anyone denies Jesus, he denies the Father who has sent Him."

Luther said: "For if I understood these words in faith—that the God who holds heaven and earth in His hand is my Father—I would conclude that therefore I am lord of heaven and earth, therefore Christ is my brother, therefore all things are mine, Gabriel is my servant, Raphael is my coachman, and all the other angels are ministering spirits sent forth by my Father in heaven to serve me in all my necessitites" (Luther's Works 54:9).

## Reflections

Read Isaiah 6:1–8. Any man who has come into the presence of the Lord realizes two things: first, the intense and overwhelming holiness of God, and secondly, the uncleanness and sinfulness of his or her own person. Peter experienced this with Jesus. He exclaimed on his knees after his marvelous catch of fish, "Go away from me, Lord; I am a sinful man!" (Luke 5:8b). No longer do you say, "Have mercy on me, a sinner" (Luke 18:13), just because it is the thing you should say. Instead you find yourself saying it because you actually can say nothing else. Your best dress of goodness looks like filthy rags. Your mouth becomes dumb. Your soul trembles with awe. Your ears hear the chant in tones you

→

have yet to hear, "Holy, holy, holy is the Lord God Almighty" (Revelation 4:8).

Read Hosea 11: 1–9. God is speaking to His beloved people, Israel, and us as well, as we like Israel tend to forget Him. At confirmation God seems close and real. We pledge ourselves for life unto the Lord. It all seems appropriate and wonderful. But perhaps over the years we find ourselves getting tired of God. "The more I called them, the more they went from Me" (verse 2). The great God kindly reminds us of our Christian training (verses 3–4). He talks out loud to Himself, asking questions that only He—God—can answer (verse 8). God is the Holy One. Yet He is the One who is Love. He desires for us to walk with Him in the paths of righteousness that He has prepared for us. Fortunately God is not a human (verse 9). We must never compare God with ourselves. God is God and nothing less. Because God is God and not man, He has loved us with an undying love and adopted us graciously into His family, bought with the price of His Son.

## "I believe in God, the Father Almighty, Maker of heaven and earth"

The creed now takes you by the hand and leads you on a quick trip through all of God's creation. It makes you look at everything God has made. You must look at the universe with its thousands of galaxies and suns that outnumber the grains of sand on the seashore. God seems unfathomable when you realize the immensity of space.

God is bigger than all of this!

The creed also makes you look in the opposite direction. You probe those parts of creation that are too small for humans to see—microbes, atoms, and DNA strands, each with its own function, and order, each turning, twisting, and doing its task according to its Designer. God becomes more unfathomable when you realize the minute intricacies of life and matter.

God is beyond all of this!

But this is not exactly what the Christian confession means when it says, "Maker of heaven and earth." It is not just the recognition of a greater force behind nature. Even many who are not Christian admit the unavoidable reality of a Creator. As you look at everything that has been made in heaven or in earth, you confess that God, your Father, the almighty One, made this. He is not just any god, but the Triune God, the God whom you confess and believe in as your God, the One who made you, loved you, saved you, and glorified you.

A grand moment came into the lives of two little children as their dad and mom were taking them up to the mountains for summer vacation. They came to the incredible log cottage where they were going to stay. They thought that any person who could build a log cottage like this surely must be a powerful person. Then the father announced the good news. He built it. He built it for them. Their own dad was the maker of that cottage! Not just any man, but their father!

This is the joyful truth you confess. This is the faith the Spirit of God has given to you. For it is "By faith we understand that the universe was formed at God's command, so that what is seen was not made out of what was visible" (Hebrews 11:3). Your God is the

Creator. He has made all things for you. He preserves all things for you. He provides all things for you.

# Reflections

Read Psalm 8. The psalmist directs you to open your eyes and look at nature all about you. Not everyone can see what the psalmist wants you to see. For only those having eyes of faith can see God in His creation. This is the wonderful thing about true faith. You see things as you have not seen them before. You don't look at the heavens as consisting of many molecules of hydrogen, or at the earth as an accidental mass of matter, or a person as the evolved substance from an amoeba. But you look at creation and see God—God at work, creating, providing, sustaining. The realization of this makes you suddenly feel very small. You feel like saying, "Who am I that You are attentive to me?" Yet God is mindful of you. No other part of His creation has received so much of Him as you. Jesus shows us this! For more on this check out Hebrews 2:5–9.

Read Psalm 91. As you grow older and feel the uncertainties of the times, the chaotic confusion of the world, the fears that continually pester humanity, you grow to love the psalms, as the warmth of their realism hits home. In this psalm God wants you to know that He is your God who can protect you against any evil, provide for you in any need, remove from you any fear, and hear you when you are in trouble. God is all this to those who "rest in the shadow of the Almighty" (Psalm 91:1). "He defends me against all danger, and guards and protects me from all evil, and all this He does only out of fatherly, divine goodness and mercy, without any merit or worthiness in me." (SC p. 14)

## "I believe in God, the Father Almighty, Maker of heaven and earth"

You cannot speak of God as your Creator and Provider without bursting into thanksgiving. Through the song of praise the Christian begins his or her confession of faith. Such a Christian is pure and undefiled in heart. He or she has learned to praise God, and God alone. A Christian gives thanks every day that the Creator of the heavens and earth and the Redeemer of the entire world is his God. In God alone is the Christian's joy found, and in such a Christian the Lord takes pleasure. How do you praise God rightly? A Christian knows how to praise God rightly when he rejoices in God more than in His goodness; when she praises the Savior more than her salvation; when he blesses the Creator more than all His creation; when she rejoices in the Giver more than in the gift.

How selfish you would be to be thankful merely for all the good things God has given to you, for the necessities God provides and your salvation from sin and death, without rejoicing in God Himself. The real Christian with the right kind of heart gives God thanks for the sheer joy of knowing Him as his or her God, whether that person must praise God from the depths or from the heights, from the green pastures or from the shadow of death. The true believer is happy to know that God is good, even when he or she apparently never experiences it. Whether in plenty or in want, the believer can praise God just as much when he or she does not feel His goodness as when he or she does. This is the right kind of heart to confess faith in the triune God, saying, "I seek not what is Yours, but You."

Every young person must learn to confess his or her faith with praise—thinking not just of the power of God or the goodness of God, but instead of the God who is all-powerful and the God who would freely give us all. This is a strong and content faith. It is a faith that ties you to God for what He is, not merely for what He does for you.

This is what Martin Luther says, "All this He does only out of fatherly, divine goodness and mercy, without any merit or worthiness in me. For all this it is my duty to thank and praise, serve and obey Him. This is most certainly true." (*SC* p. 14)

# Reflections

Read Psalm 103. The psalmist, David, addresses his own soul. He awakens it to its joyful duty of praising the Lord. David reminds us not to be forgetful of God's goodness or to take for granted His forgiveness. A thankful heart is never bitter, does not fret, is never resentful, and does not worry. How do you have a thankful heart? The psalmist tells you— recall to your mind the salvation God has given you. Here God's true greatness is revealed to those who believe. And it centers in the forgiveness of sins. Ask yourself, "Would I want God to deal with me according to my sins, my mis-

→

takes, or my failures?" If He did, you would have no future nor any hope. How are you certain that He "knows how we are formed, He remembers that we are dust" (103:14)? You must answer: "I am certain because of His Son. Jesus has become human like me. He has died my death. He has crushed the power of sin. He has been raised for my justification. His love is greater than my sin and His concern greater than my faithlessness." Because of this we have a great cause to "thank and praise, serve and obey" our God (explanation to the First Article).

Read Philippians 4:4–7. God does not need your thank-yous. But He knows that you need the joy of thanking Him. The Christian who delights in his Lord will not forget Him. The young man whose joy is Christ will not walk on the path of sin. The young woman who rejoices in her Savior will not let anxiety prevail. Those with thankful hearts receive that peace of God that surpasses human understanding. "Godliness with contentment is great gain," wrote Paul in 1 Timothy 6:6. But in our day and age few have this contentment because few have learned the Lord's gift of being thankful. Don't let certain times of the day, such as when you get up, sit down to eat, or lie down to sleep, pass without reminding yourself to give the Lord thanks. You need this gift of being thankful to Him who would in Jesus give you all things. Read again very thoughtfully St. Paul's words in Philippians 4:4–7.

## "I believe in Jesus Christ"

Jesus is the Center of our holy faith. In Him we know God the Father. In Him we know the Father's love for us. In Him we receive the life of the Holy Spirit. You cannot confess the Christian faith without speaking about Jesus. People who omit Christ, yet confess a Christian faith are actually saying something about nothing. These people may lead devotions, but their faith usually has empty thoughts because it is Jesus who is the Beginning, End, and Center of our faith.

To believe "in" Jesus Christ is one thing; to believe something "about" Jesus Christ is another. Many people believe something "about" Jesus. They believe that He was a great person, a good man, a wonderful example. Many people who go to church regularly only believe something about Jesus. They believe that the statements the church confesses about Jesus are true. They believe that such Scriptural statements are true when they say Jesus did many miracles, raised the dead, and healed the sick. They would shout a loud "Amen" to the statement "Jesus is the Son of God."

But to believe something "about" Jesus is not what you confess in this creed. You are confessing, "I believe *in* Jesus Christ." This is not a mere statement of knowledge; this is a confession of commitment. It is not just repeating something you have been taught; it is a conviction of an absolute fact. It is the expression of total trust.

Every time you say, "I believe in Jesus Christ," you are telling people that you believe that Jesus is the only Way to heaven. If you feel there are some other ways, then you do not believe *in* Jesus Christ. You are saying that Jesus is the Truth. All truth is summed up in Him, and outside of Him there exists only the deceptive lie of Satan. You are saying that Jesus is the Life. This means that your life is so bound up in Him that He actually is living in you by faith; thus St. Paul speaks true words: "The life I now live in the body, I live by faith in the Son of God" (Galatians 2:20).

# Reflections

Read 1 John 5:13–21. This portion of John's first letter has been called "The Certainties." Notice how certain we can be of what we "know." A Christian must not just "think" he or she has eternal life, or just "hope" that he or she belongs to God, but the Christian should *know*. Discover the following truths:

*The certainty of my salvation*

*The certainty of prayer*

*The certainty of overcoming evil*

*The certainty of my future*

*The certainty in the present*

*The certainty of the true God*

Use the following study to see that to believe in Jesus Christ means *life*, and to refuse Jesus Christ means *death*. There is no middle road leading to God. It is either-or. Jesus cannot be taken lightly by any individual. Literally everything depends upon Him. How important it is to believe in Jesus Christ with a surrendered heart, a humble mind, and a dedicated soul!

| If you believe in Jesus you have LIFE | | If you reject Jesus you have DEATH |
| --- | --- | --- |
| John 3:18 not condemned | | condemned already |
| John 3:36 believers—life | either-or | unbelievers—wrath |
| John 4:14 never thirst | | always thirst |
| John 8:12 the light of life | | darkness |
| John 8:24 unless you believe | | you die in sin |

## "I believe in Jesus Christ"

What is your picture of Jesus? Artists have painted their ideas on canvas throughout the centuries. Each artist paints Jesus a bit differently. The artist of Africa paints Him with African features; the artist from Japan gives Him Asian features. You paint Jesus in your mind usually as a man with a lovely beard and a halo dancing above His head. But is this Jesus? What is Jesus really like? This is not just a game. It is important that you picture Jesus as He truly is. You may not be an artist, but you already have a picture of Him in your mind. How accurate is your picture? Suppose you could be put into a time machine and go back twenty centuries to the shores of Galilee. You would see a crowd gathered about a man who you soon discover is Jesus. As you edge through the outer ring of the crowd, what would you expect to see? More important—what would this Jesus be like? Would you be disappointed like Herod, or confused like Nicodemus, or excited like Andrew? This is not a game. You must get to know Jesus.

Clear aside your present picture of Jesus. Start as best you can with a clean canvas. Then let men who actually saw Him tell you what Jesus is really like. Men like Matthew, Mark, John, and Peter all have an angle of the portrait for you. Mark, for instance, uses a quick, sharp stroke with his brush, letting you see Jesus' many emotions. Matthew brings out Jesus' kingly features. Luke emphasizes Jesus as a true Friend of sinners. John lets you see the Son of God as a real human being. As the picture becomes clearer, Jesus' eyes arrest your attention. His strides make you walk quickly just to keep up with Him. He can be entirely serious one moment and be smiling the next. With children He laughs, perhaps mending their broken toys with a carpenter's experienced hand.

Jesus was human. He grew up from a little baby as every person does—except without sin. He went through puberty. He became a teenager, living with many other teenagers His own age. At thirty He entered His formal ministry.

You are saying in the creed, "I believe that this Jesus is the Christ, the Son of God, and my only Master and Savior." You cannot confess this from the heart and walk away from Jesus. When men like Peter, Philip, James, and the rest confessed Jesus as their Lord, they wanted to follow Him. Confession and discipleship are truly one and the same.

"I believe in Jesus Christ. . . . " What is your picture of Jesus? Let the four evangelists help you. Get out a clean canvas. Pray. Begin painting.

# Reflections

Read carefully the Gospel of Mark and look specifically for descriptions and observations of Jesus that will help you picture Him more clearly. Mark writes in the style of a newspaper reporter, giving you short but sharp observed facts about Jesus. Give special attention to such passages as 1:41, 4:38, 5:43, 8:12, 10:14–16, 10:21, and 10:32. Since most of us are not overly talented with a brush and canvas, it may be helpful to write down some of Jesus' characteristics, actions, emotions, and features. Do you honestly like the picture you get? It should not be exactly the one you began with. If you have the ambition, read Luke next, then John and Matthew. See Jesus for who He really is.

Study the first eighteen verses of the Gospel of St. John. Most of what John says in his Gospel is condensed into this brief statement. These eighteen verses are called the Prologue. As you read them, you not only get a picture of the whole book, but you also get a clear, penetrating, and profound picture of Jesus. Take a pencil and write down the answer to the following:

| Read | Answer |
|------|--------|
| 1. verses 1–3 | Who He was |
| 2. verses 4–9 | Why He came |
| 3. verses 10–11 | How He was received |
| 4. verses 12–13 | What He gives |
| 5. verses 14–18 | What He revealed |

## "I believe in Jesus Christ . . . who was conceived by the Holy Spirit"

The conception of Jesus Christ was not just wonderfully holy, but it was divinely mysterious. The Christian creed progresses from one mystery to another, each needed to be accepted by faith, because no logic or human reason can explain them. The Incarnation reveals a mystery. You confess an unexplainable wonder when you say that God actually became human. You must not flinch at this wonder, for the rest of the Christian creed hinges on this truth.

How gently the creed leads us to the manger itself! We see before us the Holy One of God—the mystery of it all! At the beginning of time, Jesus already was—He existed; at the manger, Jesus is—fully human living with the human world. Right before us we see eternity squeezed into time; the Infinite packaged into our history. Our faith begins to falter, and we hesitate to look any longer. How can this be—He who holds together the cosmos now so tiny that He cannot hold up a piece of hay? It takes much faith to enter the stable, because you find that you are standing before heaven itself.

There are many things that men know to be true, but they are beyond human comprehension. A mathematician knows that "a" to the fourth power exists, but he cannot comprehend it. He can comprehend "a" to the first power; he can comprehend "a" to the second and third power. But he cannot comprehend "a" to the fourth power, yet he knows that "a" to the fourth power exists. We do not have any heavenly mathematical formula for the almighty God. Though He is incomprehensible, yet in Jesus Christ He became comprehensible to all those who believe in Him. God came all the way into our realm so that we who know and love Him might someday come into His eternal realm.

Therefore in the Christian creed we confess that Jesus Christ was conceived in the woman not by man but by the Holy Spirit. And as we confess this truth, we stand in awe at the mystery of the incarnate Christ. Yet we cannot get lost in the mystery. Scripture doesn't. The inspired writers tell us it happened. This is the important thing—it happened. God became human. He became a child to save you. And we must become children to be saved. For it is only the faith of a child that can believe the wonders of the incarnate God, Jesus Christ.

# Reflections

Think about the following portion of John's Gospel. Jesus can never be thought of in total independence of the Father, nor may the Father be thought of in total independence of the Son. To do this demonstrates all lack of understanding the Holy Trinity. Jesus said, "I and the Father are one" (John 10:30). Study the following and note the significant relationship between God the Father and God the Son:

| | | |
|---|---|---|
| John 5:19b | —"whatever the Father does the Son also does" | —for His action is the same as His Father's |
| John 5:20 | —"For the Father loves the Son and shows Him all . . ." | —for His Father has given Him the full revelation of God |

| John 5:21 | —"For just as the Father raises the dead and gives them life, even so the Son gives life to whom He is pleased to give it" | —for through Jesus humanity has life |
| John 5:22 | —For "the Father judges no one, but has entrusted all judgment to the Son" | —for all judgment has been given to the Son |

Think about the first three verses of John's Gospel. Jesus is called the "Word." This happens again in verses 14–18. Jesus is called the "Word" for a purpose. Read Genesis 1 and see how the worlds were made, then compare with John 1:3. How did God speak to men in the Old Testament? See Hebrews 1:1–2. How has God chosen to speak and reveal Himself to us today? For that answer see John 1:18. It can be said that Jesus Christ is the final revelation of God to the world and therefore John correctly calls Him "the Word." If any individual or any religious body claims to receive additional revelations from God for their doctrine, what does this do to Jesus? Give this serious thought, and give God thanks for the fullness of His revelation, His love, His life, His wisdom that you can have by faith in Jesus Christ. Little wonder that God says to us, "This is My Son, whom I love; with Him I am well pleased. Listen to Him!" (Matthew 17:5).

## "I believe in Jesus Christ . . .
## born of the Virgin Mary"

These words invite us first to look at the Child and then to look at
His mother. Sometimes we may become so overwhelmed at the
divinity of the Lord Jesus that we fail to appreciate His humanity. A
noted professor once said, "Christians find it easier to believe that
Jesus Christ is true God than true man." Yet Jesus was human. He
came into this world, as did you and I, through the womb of a
human mother. In this lies the beauty of the words, "I believe in
Jesus Christ . . . born of the Virgin Mary."

Rejoice in this truth—that Jesus was human in every respect as
we are, except He did not have the stain of sin. He identified
Himself with us to be the only true representative of all humanity.
He became like one of us so that He could call you His brother or
His sister. He did not become a part of any other of His creation.
God became human in Jesus Christ. No wonder that angels should
marvel at this! Jesus was so much a part of us that He could actually
take upon Himself our sin, share our death, and fight our hell. As
you look at the Child on Mary's lap, rejoice at the wonder of it all,
then thank God for the reality of it all.

Rejoice in the humanity of your Lord Jesus.

## Reflections

Study the following references to the birth of Jesus
Christ. Each one will give you real understanding of the
Incarnation.

→

1. Read Matthew 1 and 2. As you read, look for the significance of Jesus' genealogy, for example, why did Jesus have to be "the Son of David and the Son of Abraham"? Why does Matthew emphasize the virgin birth of Jesus (1:18–25)? After reading chapter two, look up Isaiah 60:1–6. Note the relationship and give a reason why this Isaiah text is read on Epiphany.

2. Read Luke 1 and 2:1–20. Read the song of Mary (1:46–55); the song of Zechariah (1:67–79); and the song of the angels (2:14). Mary praises God for what He is; Zechariah praises God for what He does; and the angels praise God for both what He is and what He can give mankind.

Study again the Christmas story, this time in John 1:14. It has been called the most profound statement on the living form of our Lord. To rightly grasp the fullness of these words, you must compare John 1:14 with John 1:1. It may help to make a list so that you can see how these two descriptions of Christ come together. Both verses have three parts. On your list make two columns. On the top of one write verse one; and on top of the other write verse fourteen. In the first write the three parts of the first verse in order. In the second write the three parts of the fourteenth verse also in order. Now you can see the first part of verse one parallel to the first part of verse fourteen, i.e., "In the beginning was the Word" (v. 1) ... "And the Word became flesh" (v. 14). The "Word" is Jesus. See how close God comes to us. He is no longer "way out there," but in Jesus Christ, God is here with us, eating, drinking, dwelling, talking, and sleeping with us.

## "I believe in Jesus Christ . . .
## who suffered under Pontius Pilate"

No other man in history has his name repeated as often and by as many as does Pontius Pilate. Yet no man envies him his reputation, for every time his name is spoken, it is linked with the killing of God's Son. God's Son suffered under Pontius Pilate.

Yet it is beneficial that the name of such a man is part of the creed of the church. Every time you confess the faith and repeat his name, you realize that the crucifying of God's Son is part of human history. It is not a figment of man's imagination. It is not the product of a tragic legend. It is history—our history. At a specific time in history God chose to send His Son. History can be called a picture of the life of all humankind. At the very center of this picture, God planted a cross to reveal the utter blackness of man's sin and to reveal at the same time the inexpressible love of God.

The decision of Pilate and the murderous cries of the mob are not something only of yesterday, something that happened over 2,000 years ago, but rather Pilate's decision is human reason and the decision of what to do with God's righteousness in comparison to our humanity. Every age has to confront the same question as did Pilate, "What shall I do with Jesus?" Every denial of truth, every act of injustice, every rejection of purity is a repetition of Pilate's decision. No one can escape the silent figure of Jesus, just standing in the judgment hall of people's decisions, waiting for the verdict. Look into history and look hard! What has been man's continual verdict? It is spelled out in every sin of mankind—"Crucify Him! Away with Him!"

Every time you say the name of Pontius Pilate in the creed of the church, look into his face, and you may see your own. How close Pilate's problem is to your own!

"Should I cheat on the next exam?" "Should I tell a lie to my parents?" "Should I lose my virginity before I am married?" "Should I drink at the party on Friday night?" You condemn Pilate, and rightly so. But what about yourself? Don't excuse Pilate, and don't excuse yourself either. The Son of God hanging on the cross permits no excuse.

"What shall I do with Jesus?" You can't get rid of Jesus, for He is a real part of our history. "What shall I do with Him?" The question is still with us. Your answer adds another page to man's history.

## Reflections

Read John 18:33 through 19:16. Study Pontius Pilate and note his willingness to do what was right, but his lack of determination to carry it through. Knowing what is right and having the spiritual courage to do it are two different things. You need both to be a faithful child of God. Don't look only at Pontius Pilate, but study Jesus also. Listen carefully to Jesus' answers. Jesus says in 18:37 that He was born to rule men in truth. As Jesus rules your life, you find the kingdom of God. Jesus says in John 19:11 that power comes from God alone. In today's age of power—nuclear power, political power, economic power, and media power—we must be constantly reminded of this truth. Power does not come

→

from people alone. When people have power, it is something given to them by God.

Read the second chapter of Hebrews. See the perfect identification of Jesus with mankind. Jesus took His place not apart or outside of our human race, but at its very center, so that the burden of the world's guilt would gather up and roll upon Him. Jesus became one with Judas and Pilate; one with Caiaphas and the spitting soldiers; one with Caesar and Hitler; one with you and me. But in what sense? Memorize Hebrews 2:14–15.

### "I believe in Jesus Christ . . . crucified!"

The cross of Jesus is the symbol of our holy faith. By means of this cross God actually reconciled the world unto Himself again. The fact of the cross tells us clearly this is God's way of bringing us back into the sphere of life again. The cross is like a key, unlocking both the mind and the heart of God. It unlocks the mind of the Almighty One, unleashing His piercing thoughts on our sin. God hates sin! But it also unlocks the heart of the Almighty One, revealing a love that surpasses our highest thoughts. God loves us!

It was not the nails that held Jesus on that first Good Friday; nor was it the hatred of the mobs or Pilate's order. They all thought they held Him. What really bound Jesus? Love for you. Love for me. This is what bound Him to be sacrificed as the Lamb of God slain from the foundation of the world. It was not the power of men that bound Jesus to that cross. It was the eternal and seeking love of God.

As you repeat these words, repeat them slowly and somberly, "I believe in Jesus Christ . . . crucified." Naked as He had come from God He went to God, taking nothing with Him that was human but only the load of humanity's sin. Look at your Savior fastened to a tree of your making. See His sacred hands nailed to the crossbeam: hands of the Carpenter; hands hardened with toil; hands that healed the sick and blessed the children; hands that held five small loaves and multiplied them for the 5,000; saving hands that reached out to Peter sinking in the sea; holy hands that were constantly lifted up to the Father in prayer that His holy will might be done. Now they are bleeding hands, pierced through with the sins of men and held outstretched with the unbelief of the world. Their outstretched position still signals all men to come into the kingdom of heaven, and the dripping blood still cleanses us from all our sin.

Tell me in what else can you find glory except in the cross of Christ, your Lord? Where else can you find the forgiveness of sins and the everlasting peace of God for your soul? Now look at your own hands—your feet, your tongue as well. Your hands that perform so much evil, yet which you wish would perform nothing but good. In Christ crucified there is the strength to work for those things that are good. He cleanses and makes all things like new.

## Reflections

Study 1 Corinthians 1:18–31. God chose the preaching of the Cross as His means of saving people. This message to some is an absurdity; but to others it is the power of God. Why is the message of the Cross an absurdity to some?

Because it strips them of their wisdom, their own righteousness, and their pride of power. It demands a contrite heart, a repentant mind, and a surrendered soul. Perhaps this illustration will help you grasp the meaning of this Bible study. Recall the story of the great ship Titanic. It sailed on its maiden voyage across the Atlantic with the title "The Unsinkable." Not heeding the iceberg warnings, it plowed into one which led to its destruction. The captain and the designer awoke to the unbelievable fact that the ship would sink and ordered the lifeboats to be lowered right away. But many of the people refused to get into the lifeboats, for they felt more secure on their "unsinkable" ship than in such flimsy craft. As a result many perished as the "unsinkable" sank. The point of this illustration lies in the lifeboats. To those who were perishing, they were utter folly. But to those who were being saved, they were the method for their salvation. So, too, to those who are on the road to destruction, the Cross is utter foolishness, but to those who are being saved, it manifests the real power and the true wisdom of God.

Read Isaiah 53. Someone has said that the prophet was closer to the cross on that first Good Friday than any of the evangelists. It is a wonder that a man like Isaiah living many centuries before Christ could paint such an intimate and personal picture of the crucifixion. As you read this chapter, in place of the "He" put "Jesus," and in place of the plural "our" and "we" put your own name. See how closely Christ's death becomes your death. See how real and personal His atoning death is for you. Read Romans 6:1–11 and see how through Jesus' death on the cross you can (by faith) be dead to sin and be alive to God!

## "I believe in Jesus Christ . . . who died and was buried"

People come into this world only to die. With all their cultural and scientific advances, humans still have to die. We are told that we are living longer today than our grandparents did. The age span is lengthening more each decade. Yet no matter how many years one gains for life on this little planet, death still waits patiently to receive the individual into its cold arms. Death plays no favorites. Whether you are rich or poor, beautiful or ugly, smart or slow, drive a BMW or use public transportation, death is the common end of us all.

If death meant only extinction; if death meant only that I would no longer exist, then I could eat, drink, and party, for tomorrow we disappear from the universe. But the Scriptures, our Lord Jesus, and our inner souls tell us that the placing of six feet of dirt over a body or turning it into ash is not the end. Death is not just being cut off from the land of the living. Death is being cut off from eternal life with God.

Jesus said in a parable that if a strong man has many possessions, he can keep all that he has until one stronger than he comes. When the stronger one comes, the man will be overcome. Jesus is the "Stronger One." No man has overcome death, nor can he. But there has come into our world One stronger than death. In Jesus Christ our death is actually buried. No longer are we separated from the life of God. As Jesus Himself promised, "Whoever believes in [Me] shall not perish!"

Stop as you say these words, "I believe in Jesus Christ . . .who died and was buried." In respect be silent before the tomb. Let your tears flow as you see the sinless One of God being laid in your tomb and bearing your death. What a cruel and undeserved death this is! Yet give God thanks that it happened. Now there need not be any more fear of death nor the tomb because Christ has brought our salvation. "Where, grave, thy victory?" ("Abide with Me" *LW* 490).

Now—right now—give God thanks for the victory that is yours in the Lord Jesus Christ.

# Reflections

Study the following table. This may prove both interesting and helpful. The sacrificial death of our Lord was a necessary way for God to reconcile the world unto Himself. It was no accident. Beginning centuries before Christ Jesus was born into our world, God was educating His people to the idea of atonement for sin. The picture God used was that of a lamb.

## Jesus, the Lamb

| | | |
|---|---|---|
| • Abraham's lamb (ram) | • Genesis 22:13 | • shows God providing |
| • The Passover lamb | • Exodus 12:5 | • shows it must die |
| • The Levitical lamb | • Leviticus 22:19–20 | • shows it must have no blemish |
| • The sacrificed lamb | • Leviticus 23:19 | • shows it is for sin |

### Jesus as the Lamb

| | | |
|---|---|---|
| • The prophet Isaiah | • Isaiah 53:7 | • identifies the "lamb" to be a man |
| • John the Baptist | • John 1:29 | • identifies Jesus Christ as the Lamb of God (completing the picture) |
| • John in his Revelation | • Revelation 7:9 and 15:3 | • shows us the victorious Lamb |

Read Romans 5. St. Paul is known for his clear statements on the doctrine of justification by faith. As you read, note the following:

1. Peace with God must come before you can talk about peace of mind; see verses 1 and 2. And peace with God comes only through our Lord Jesus Christ.

2. Note what Paul calls us, namely, "sinners," "ungodly," and "enemies." What does this say about our former relationship with God? What does this tell you about God's love in Jesus?

3. Paul compares Christ and Adam in this chapter. In order to best understand the comparison, it may be helpful to make a list of their descriptions. Making two columns, title one "Christ" and the other "Adam." List in the respective columns what is said of Christ and Adam, and note the relationship between the two. In Christ we see grace for all; in Adam we see death for all. By the Holy Spirit pray that you apprehend the riches of God's grace.

### "I believe in Jesus Christ . . . . He descended into hell. The third day He rose again from the dead"

Jesus is not just a figure in a book. If Jesus had not risen from the dead, you probably would not have heard of Him. But Jesus rose! This means you believe in a living, victorious Lord. Jesus is not just a symbol of immortality. He is not just another beautiful expression of springtime. Jesus is alive. He is as alive today as when He walked on the Sea of Galilee.

There is no spiritual resurrection here. It is the resurrection of Jesus Christ who hung on the cross. It is not a recalling of a beautiful memory of the grandest man who ever lived. On the third day God raised up Jesus Christ's body. And when God raised Jesus from the dead, He ushered in the beginning of the new age of the kingdom of heaven.

As you know, there are two sides to a coin. One side you usually call "heads," the other "tails." You cannot speak about one side without speaking about the other, because it takes both sides to make the coin. If you could take one side of the coin away—for instance the "tails"—you would actually destroy the coin. Similarly, you cannot speak about Good Friday without speaking about Easter. You cannot speak about the crucifixion without also speaking of the resurrection. The two are two sides of God's great act of atonement for sin and for His victory over hell and death. Therefore, as one Lutheran theologian has said, you must speak about the crucifixion-resurrection. The crucifixion was not a defeat that had to be fixed by the resurrection, but rather the crucifixion was God's victory over sin and death, which is proved beyond any doubt by the resurrection.

Look at the world into which you must go. The world with its chaos, its uncertainty, its anxiety, its fears, its death, its hell, its helplessness, its sin. It often appears to be one huge picture of Good Friday. As St. Paul declares, if the rulers of this age had known the wisdom of God, they would not have crucified the Lord of Glory.

Look at the other side of the coin. See Jesus Christ, your Savior, as the risen Lord. In Jesus all things will become new. In Jesus, God ushers in the new age. You are part of the new age of God because you belong to Jesus Christ. You are "more than conquerors" (Romans 8:37) in your risen Lord.

# Reflections

Skim through the Book of Acts. True, this will take a little time, but your effort will be rewarding. Notice, maybe even underline, all of the references to the resurrection of Jesus Christ. See if it is not true that everything in the Book of Acts hinges on the fact that God raised Jesus Christ from the dead. Pay attention to the importance of the resurrection in the many sermons and speeches throughout the book. Finally, see how the word "witness," one of the key words in Acts, usually is used in connection to the resurrection of Jesus. This should say something to you about the power of a true witness to Jesus in your own life.

Read 1 Corinthians 15:1–20. This chapter is generally known as the "Resurrection Chapter." The reason is obvious. It discusses the importance and meaning of Christ's resurrection for the resurrection of all believers in Christ. Note two things as you study this section. First, notice the number of witnesses to whom Jesus appeared after His resurrection. It was not small. Compare verse 9 with Acts 9:3–6. This incident is most important to Paul. Second, what is Paul's argument in verses 12–19. Do you think it valid? Do you agree with Paul's statements in verses 17 and 19? Does this help you understand the joy of knowing Jesus Christ as your risen Lord?

Compare Romans 1:4 with 1:16. Note the word "power" in both verses. The power of God in the Gospel of Jesus Christ is that power in the resurrection of Jesus Christ. Because of the resurrection of Jesus Christ from the dead, the Gospel is the power of God. Thank God you know this Gospel.

## "I believe in Jesus Christ . . . who ascended into heaven and sits at the right hand of God, the Father Almighty"

We think a lot of names. The "little kid" in each of us makes us impressed with big names. We think of the big names in the movie scene, the big names in government, the big names in sports, even the big names in our history books—scientists, explorers, and writers. There are many big, famous names. Some stars are famous for their talent, while others are known for their "15 seconds of fame." Some names we associate with hateful actions. Even the bad names are famous. With a big name, things happen. And generally fame, power, and wealth follow.

Now there is a name that is above every other name on earth or in heaven. Before this name all other names are as nothing, for they all kneel in adoration before it. There is one name that is called the "name that is above every name" (Philippians 2:9b) and this name is Jesus Christ.

Jesus' ascension into heaven declares that He has this name. God the Father has given Jesus this name above all names. So happy is the Father with His only begotten Son that He is only too willing to give to Jesus Christ that title that is above any other in the cosmos. That is why there is no other name under heaven given among men by which they can be eternally saved. It is about this name that John writes, "On His robe and on His thigh He has this name written, King of kings and Lord of lords" (Revelation 19:16).

Praise God that you know this name. Thank God that in His grace He has bound you to this name.

*May every heart confess Your name*

*Forever You adore*

*And, seeking You, itself inflame*

*To seek You more and more!*

"O Jesus, King Most Wonderful" *LW* 274:4

Thus the ascension of our Lord Jesus Christ and His sitting at the right hand of the Father make us look up and rejoice. He rules this hectic world with you in mind, and you confess His name. He carries you when your problems become heavy and your faith becomes weak. He promises and sends the Holy Spirit to help you know what is true and false, right and wrong. He is eager to return for you and bring you to where He now, so that the glorification of the name of God can be complete.

When you confess, "I believe in Jesus Christ . . . who ascended into heaven and sits at the right hand of God, the Father Almighty," say it with eyes looking upward and with a spirit proud of this name above all names. After all, in this name you shall stand some-day before God as His child.

# Reflections

Study Philippians 2:5–11. To appreciate Christ's exaltation, you must first understand Christ's humiliation. The truth that Christ has ascended and now sits at the right hand of the Father can be best understood in the person and work of

Christ for our salvation. Consider following comparison between Christ and the old Adam.

| Adam | Jesus Christ |
|---|---|
| • made in the image of God, | • being in the form of God, |
| • thought it a prize to be grasped at | • thought it not a prize to be grasped at |
| • to be as god; | • to be like God, |
| • he strove to be of reputation | • but made Himself of no reputation |
| • and spurned being God's servant, | • and took upon Him the form of a servant |
| • wishing to be in the likeness of God; | • and was made in the likeness of men; |
| • and being found in fashion as a man, | • and being found in fashion as a man, |
| • he exalted himself | • He humbled Himself |
| • and was disobedient unto death. | • and became obedient unto death, even the death of the cross. |

Therefore God exalted Him to the highest place and gave Him the name which is above every name, that at the name of Jesus every knee should bow... Philippians 2:10–11a

God exalted Jesus because He did for you what you were unable to do for yourself, namely, He has bought for you eternal life, the forgiveness of sins, and all things to work for your salvation.

→

Read Colossians 3:1–4 and Philippians 3:12–14. American society can become horribly materialistic, worldly, and bound to the desires of this earth. This is dangerous. It can ground your vision and quench your faith. This may account for your many evil and dirty thoughts, your slanderous and cutting tongue, and your sinful, rebellious actions. Your old sinful nature (old Adam) and your sanctified new man are at war within you as your old nature struggles to live in this world and your new nature wants to confess Christ. As we remember our baptism and what Christ has done for us, we live sanctified—we live our lives for Christ. With this in mind, read slowly Colossians 3:1–4. To confess the ascended Christ means you have to live "upstairs." Now this is no flight into unreality, but rather a good look at reality for the first time. Sanctified, made holy by Christ, we live our lives waiting for the time, when we too will be with Christ in heaven.

## "I believe in Jesus Christ . . . . He will come to judge the living and the dead"

The movie, *The Matrix*, gives one the image of a world so dark that one is depressed at the real world. The characters and viewers, alike, desire to escape into a fantasy world. This dark world, where death is around every corner and the images of beauty and imagination crumble into the darkness of reality causes us fear. Not fear that there are machines using our bodies for fuel, but fear that this world is not all that it was cracked up to be. At times we, like the characters in movies, want to run from a world that seems too dark, too awful to be true, a world where it is hard to imagine that God exists, and even harder to see Him in control. The media and movies give us such storylines, but we sympathize with the character that runs in fear of such a scary world.

You felt like running many times. Perhaps you have. The world looks scary and God far away. You looked at the great plan of the Kingdom and think it impossible. You listen to the Gospel promises and think them foolish. Thinking that God is no longer around, or if He is, He doesn't care, you run. You run looking for something to give you an answer in this hectic world.

Every Christian reacts like Peter at one time or another. We see the evil people triumph over the good people. We see children dying in the streets because of terrorist attacks. We see injustice and immorality overrunning the respectable and the pure.

The world with its billions of people and with its maze of sin looks like a giant jigsaw puzzle scattered hopelessly over the board of time. No wonder you are not sure where you fit sometimes. You ask, What is the answer to everything people do and everything people are? You ask, Where and when is everything going to be added up so that the final answer to the life of men can be seen?

It is in this statement of the creed, "I believe in Jesus Christ . . . [who] will come to judge the living and the dead." Jesus will give you and everybody else the final answer to everything humanity has or has not done in this world. Jesus will come again to reveal the perfect and stunning judgment of the almighty God.

"I am the Alpha and the Omega," says the Lord God. In God all things began. In God all things shall find their completion. Those who believe will find the completion of their faith, which is eternal life with God. Those who do not believe will find the completion of their unbelief, which is eternal death.

Take comfort and encouragement in this fact that your Lord Jesus Christ will bring everything to a final conclusion. Oftentimes, we look to find completion in our own lives. We look to our friends, to love, to a career that will define who we are. But we are not our friends, our romantic interests, or our jobs. We are God's. In Him we find completion. Our Lord of completeness completes us, fulfills us. Our God of completeness rules this world and will complete it in His time. Take comfort that the Lord Jesus still rules the heavens—and the earth too.

# Reflections

Ponder this biblical truth. A person has life when he believes in Jesus Christ. The individual is judged and condemned to death. If one does not accept Jesus, he or she is already condemned. When the individual dies, he or she will be resurrected to eternal judgment. Answer the following:

1. When is an individual confronted with the decision of believing or not believing? (See John 9:35 and following)

2. When does life begin? (See John 5:24)

3. When does judgment begin? (See John 3:16–21)

4. When is the final judgment? (See John 5:28–29)

Judgment is not just something happening *to* us, but something happening *in* us. For example, a student fails the final exam. This is not the student's real judgment. The student's actual judgment arises from his or her daily refusal to study, so that all the student's life he or she must suffer from the punishment of laziness and ignorance. So, too, when an individual, confronted by God in His Gospel, does not believe, he places himself under condemnation and God's wrath from that moment forward to all eternity.

Study John 17. This chapter reflects the joy that filled Jesus' heart and every Christian's. This joy anticipates Jesus' second coming in glory.

## Joy

| | |
|---|---|
| The joy of speaking with the Father | 1 |
| The joy of eternal life | 3 |
| The joy of being accepted by God | 6 and 8 |
| The joy of knowing that our Lord prays for us | 9 |
| The joy of being kept by the Father | 11 |
| The joy of knowing His joy | 13 |
| The joy of separation | 14–17 and 19 |
| The joy of being sent | 18 |
| The joy of fellowship with God and believers | 21–23 |
| The joy of future glory | 24 |
| The joy of knowing God's love | 26 |

## "I believe in the Holy Spirit"

Spirit? Ghost? It sounds like the topic of a scary story or some unbelievable lie. "I believe in the Holy Spirit" may sound like this to some people, but they are totally mistaken. The Holy Spirit is not like this at all. He is not a mysterious person, though He is a person. He is not a strange force that can be somehow measured like electricity, though He is Power. He is not a substance that can be placed into a test tube and measured, though He can be "seen." He cannot be detected by the five senses, yet He can be felt. The Holy Spirit is both most real and unreal: real to those who know God; unreal to those who do not.

Every time you meet the Holy Spirit in the Scriptures something is happening. In Genesis one, He appears in the second verse as the worlds are being created! And you meet Him working through people like the Old Testament prophets. Listen to those men speak with the power of the Spirit. Nineveh, a city of over a million, repents when Jonah preaches His message. You probably see Him at His finest hour on Pentecost when in flames of heavenly fire He poured out His fullness on the one hundred and twenty in the upper room. This little band of men and women turned the Roman world upside down.

The people who truly believe in the Holy Spirit are people who are open on the Godward side. What does this mean? Let's begin by stating the negative. If all a young man can think about is his car, or all a young woman can worry about is her clothes, the Holy Spirit will be unreal to both of them. If an organization deliberately or unintentionally keeps people away from Christian fellowship, then that group of young people does not have the full fellowship of the Spirit of God. On the other hand, when a young Christian finds that something makes him or her stand up for Jesus and bear witness to the truth when truth must be spoken, this is the work of the Holy Spirit. When young people can get together to talk and pray about the work of Christ in this world, this is the activity of the Holy Spirit.

The Holy Spirit works in people the desire for the Godward side. Such young people think that Jesus Christ and His Gospel are more important than anything else in their lives. Such young people will be used by God because the Holy Spirit will fill them with the power and life of God.

You say, "I believe in the Holy Spirit." Watch out! Big things can begin happening in your life too.

## Reflections

Look through portions of the Book of Acts. First, note the key verse, 1:8. Place a small key in the margin next to this verse. Then underline three basic words in this verse, which are used throughout the book: "power . . . Holy Spirit . . . witnesses." Each word can be studied separately, but let us think just on the "Holy Spirit." Skim through the following chapters and discover who He is and how He works:

**Chapter 2**—His part in God's great plan for the world

**Chapter 5**—His divine person

**Chapter 6**—His indispensable part in making men to be men of God

**Chapter 7**—His guidance in the program of the church

**Chapter 13**—His selecting, directing, and commissioning of apostles

What you see the Holy Spirit doing here in Acts, He desires to do to you and with you and through you.

Read John 16:5–15. Why is it to our advantage that Jesus ascended into heaven rather than staying here on earth? And what does all this have to do with the sending of the Holy Spirit? Look at verse 7. These verses tell us that the Holy Spirit will deal with the most basic elements of our spiritual state: sin, righteousness, and judgment. First, we see that the Spirit is He who shows us humanity's position with God, that is, that humans have fallen from God. Then the Spirit shows us the two powers that would rule us: Christ, the victorious One who has ascended to the right hand of power; and the devil, the defeated one, who has been judged and who will continue to be judged till the final Day. Christians truly believe in the Holy Spirit because He has shown them their sin, has shown the need of Christ's kind of righteousness and not humanity's, has shown them the victory that is theirs over sin, death, and hell itself because they are Christ's.

## "I believe in the Holy Spirit . . . who has called me"

Everyone likes to feel important. We like to feel wanted. It can make all the difference of night and day to be left out of the big party of the year or to be invited. You know this. We feel special when we are picked for the sports team we tried out for, or win a music or academic award, or find out someone likes us.

There is something just as exciting in the work of the Holy Spirit. He has invited you to the biggest event in eternity; He has chosen you for a team that is to carry out God's task; He has asked you of all people to walk hand in hand with the Lord Jesus Christ. This is what you say: "I believe that I cannot by my own reason or strength believe in Jesus Christ, my Lord, or come to Him; *but the Holy Spirit has called me...." (SC).* You are important, important to God and therefore very, very important.

You have been chosen before the foundation of the world to be a part of God's kingdom. You are the realization of a divine idea. In the millenniums of yesterday God thought of you, and in the realm of time He sought you out and called you into His kingdom.

Don't get the idea that the Holy Spirit called you because you are especially wise or especially foolish. He has not chosen you because you are wealthy or because you are pitifully poor. He has not called you because you are Caucasian or African American, Latino, Asian, or anything else. The Holy Spirit has called you into God's family because God loves you and all sinners like you. Because of God's love for you, the Spirit has opened your eyes to see your sin and has introduced you to Jesus as your Savior and Lord.

Don't quench, don't stop the Spirit, said Paul. Don't cut off God's heavenly food on which your faith depends. Don't block the Spirit's daily invitation to listen to your Lord speak to you in the Word. Don't minimize the glorious fact that you are actually a child of God. The Spirit's calling may seem too good to be true. It is "too good," but it happens to be very *true*.

For meditation reflect on the fact that Christians are the dear children of God because they are chosen by God. St. John in his Gospel brings this truth to the heart. We have no claim to God. He alone has a claim to us in Jesus Christ. John discusses Jesus choosing His disciples in John 1:35 and following. As you read these verses note the disciples referred to here and the word "finding" in verse 43. Compare this with 6:70 and 15:16. The word "found" does not mean here to discover by accident, but it implies the idea of "searching out." The disciples had nothing within themselves to boast of when Jesus chose them to be His disciples. No person has anything whatsoever to boast of by which he or she became a child of God. God chooses you only by a force within Himself, namely, His grace. Look up 6:65 and pay close attention to the words "no one" and "unless." You and I have come to faith only because God has given us the power to believe. Where is boasting? In 17:11 Jesus says that we were "given" to Him by God. God gave because God chose. Therefore you are truly the very chosen of God in Jesus Christ by the power of the Holy Spirit.

## Reflections

Consider the fact that you are a child of God because you belong to God. You are eternally important. This may give you self-confidence to do your schoolwork well, to obey your parents with respect, and to face the world with determination. Examine the following verses in John 10 and see why you are so important, see why you are a child of God.

→

**We are children of God because . . .**

| | |
|---|---|
| We are the sheep God speaks of | **10:1 and following** |
| We are called "His own" | **10:3–4** |
| We are known by Him individually | **10:14** |
| We are saved because He laid down His life | **10:15** |
| We are secure in God's embrace | **10:29** |

Since you belong to God in Jesus Christ, nothing in this life can separate you from Him! (See also Romans 8:37–39.)

## "I believe in the Holy Spirit . . . who has enlightened me with His gifts"

Jacob asked Tyler, "Where is the group?" Tyler responded, "They are in the locker room making big plans for this weekend." Hurriedly Jacob walks to the locker room and upon entering is greeted by his friends. They ask him to join them and make plans with them. Happy to be included in the plan, Jacob asks, "Heard you got big ideas for this weekend. Enlighten me!" As we can see, Jacob wanted to know what was going on.

When you believe in the Holy Spirit, you want to say to Him, "*Enlighten* me! Tell me the things that I should know as a member of God's family." For it is the Holy Spirit who can enlighten you with God's good gifts. One of His functions is to educate us, to free us from our lack of knowledge and mistakes, and to inform us of things that we can in no way find out by ourselves.

First understand that the Holy Spirit speaks a language entirely different from that of humans. That is why you first must be called into the "group" before you can understand what is really happening. Suppose you were traveling through a foreign country and wanted to ask a question, but the people in this country do not speak your language. Your language and their language would hardly provide a suitable meeting ground for asking or understanding your questions. What you would need is a translator's dictionary. The language of the God is never understood by any person outside of God's family group. As much as people desire to know the things of God, we simply can't understand them. In fact, when God speaks about a cross, humanity thinks it is pretty silly. But when you are called into God's family by the Holy Spirit, suddenly the cross becomes the power of God. The Holy Spirit then leads you from one truth to another, till you are listening to things that even the angels do not fully comprehend.

How does the Holy Spirit enlighten you? Through the Scriptures. Do not think that the Word of God constitutes so many vowels and consonants, so many words and sentences. But the Word of God is the very voice of the Holy Spirit, the very power of God, the very life of Jesus Christ. To understand what is going on in the mind of God, you must study the Scriptures.

"I believe in the Holy Spirit . . . [who] has called me by the Gospel [and] enlightened me with His gifts." We have enough Christians still in the dark. The Spirit is waiting for you to say with open Scripture in hand, "Dear Holy Spirit, enlighten me. Let me know what is going on when it comes to God."

# Reflections

Read the First Psalm thoughtfully. Pay close attention to verse two; reread it several times. By the "Law of the Lord" the psalmist is not just speaking about the Ten Commandments. Rather he is thinking about God's full covenant with him given through the great prophet Moses. We could translate this into the new covenant term "the Gospel of Jesus Christ." Both terms are God's Word to humanity. And the psalmist says that he "delights" in this Word. Why? Because this "Law of the Lord" is God's Word to him. It is God's message to him. David would think of no one else from whom he would rather hear than from God Himself. Let us compare this with a person madly in love. When this person opens his or her email account to find an email from the one he or she loves, this person opens it quickly and scans it, looking hurriedly at the final words to see if the other still loves him or her. The other does. Now the letter is read more slowly. Finishing it for the third time, the letter is saved. This teenager "meditates" on the email day and night. The children of God who truly love the Lord love to read and meditate on His Word to them. They honestly delight in it!

Read Psalm 119. This is a lengthy psalm, but well worth it. You may like to meditate on each of its twenty-two sections at different times during the week. Each section has eight verses. The twenty-two sections represent each letter in the Hebrew alphabet. As each letter of the Hebrew alphabet was used to declare the written and spoken Word of God, so each letter is honored by a special section of eight lines.

The entire psalm is a poem of praise about the Word of God. Every verse has a reference to it: "Law of the Lord . . . decrees . . . Your ways . . . precepts . . . statutes . . . commandments . . . ordinances." This psalm can teach you a real love for God's Word if read and reread prayerfully. Note with special interest the second section, verses 9–16, which speaks about young people.

## "I believe in the Holy Spirit . . . who has sanctified and kept me in the true faith"

To say that you believe in the sanctifying power of the Holy Spirit and not to be set apart for His purpose in God's great design would be like buying a basketball but never using it or having pair of designer jeans but never wearing them. You put a basketball to use, and you have jeans to wear, and you believe in the Holy Spirit to be set apart for the holy purpose of God.

To be sanctified by the Spirit of God is not only being set apart for something special in God's plan, but it is also being separated from something for something. Think of the example of the jeans again. You do not wear these nice, new, expensive jeans to clean your bathroom or to paint your room in. You wear these jeans for that occasion for which they were designed, for school or going out with friends. When the Holy Spirit sanctifies a person, He separates that person from everything that is not of God for everything that is of God.

The Holy Spirit does not permit you to be in two places at the same time. You can't be in sin and in the righteousness of Jesus at the same time. You can't be telling a lie and saying you love the truth at the same time. You can't belong to yourself and belong to God at the same time. You can't love money and everything money can buy and at the same time love the Lord Jesus Christ. It is the Holy Spirit who can and does separate you from the one for the other. Even as Jesus, your Lord and Savior, has separated you from sin and death for righteousness and life, so the Spirit of God continues this process till you are living completely and solely for your Father who is in heaven.

St. Paul begins his Letter to the Romans with the words, "[I have been] set apart for the Gospel of God" (1:1). This was the Spirit's work. For what has the Holy Spirit separated you? God cannot use you or any Christian unless he or she is sanctified by the Spirit. The reason why we have so few Christians separated fully unto the wonderful Gospel of the Lord Jesus is that they fight the Spirit who would set them apart for an important part in God's eternal plan.

The beauty of sanctification is that it is not ours to do. Christ, in dying on the cross and rising from the dead, set us apart to be His children. Our sinful nature rejects God, but in our Baptism we are washed free of the sin in our old sinful nature. In our daily remembrance of our Baptism, we are reminded that we are justified by Christ's actions and now sanctified and holy before His eyes.

# Reflections

Read Hebrews 11:23–28 and compare this reading with the first three chapters of Exodus. Moses is surely one of

→

the great examples of a sanctified man of God. Here is a man truly set apart by God for God's holy purpose. He was separated by the Spirit of God from everything that Egypt could offer for everything that God had planned for His people. Read carefully verses 24–26. Could you have made his great choice? By the Spirit's power you could have. Do not think it was an easy choice! Certainly Moses sweat it out in his faith.

Actually Moses gave up nothing for Jesus. Everything that Egypt had—its treasures, its power, its pleasures—the Egyptians gave up on him because he belonged to God. A noted theology teacher from Philadelphia gave this personal illustration. During one of those lovely days in spring when he was a boy, everybody was playing marbles, including himself. As he was playing, some of the big boys walked past with baseball mitts and bats, talking about the game. Suddenly one stopped and came over to him and asked, "How about playing right field for us today? One of the guys is sick." Of course, he jumped up and went along happily with the big boys, leaving the *little* boys to their marbles. He played so well that day that he was asked to play the following day too. After the game he walked with glove in hand past the "little boys" playing marbles. Marbles no longer interested him. He didn't give them up. They gave him up.

When the Holy Spirit works on an individual who loves the Lord Jesus, the individual doesn't give up anything. Rather the things of the world give the Christian up, for they no longer can attract and hold him or her.

Compare Romans 1:1 with Deuteronomy 15:12–18, giving special thought to the word "servant," or "slave." Paul calls himself a "servant of Jesus Christ." Being a Hebrew, Paul is using an Old Testament picture of a bondslave (New King James Version) as described in Deuteronomy 15:12–18. The Law of Moses stated that a Hebrew could be placed into slavery for a debt that he or she owes, but in the seventh year, known as the Sabbatic Year, he or she was to be set free. God wanted no permanent system of slavery for His own people. But if a man or woman for some reason or another desired to remain with his kind master permanently and serve the master, then the master would take a ring and thrust it through his or her ear, and that man or woman would be his bondslave forever. Paul found a new freedom in the Lord Jesus Christ, and he willingly desired to be a "bondslave" for Jesus, not because he had to, but because he wanted to.

## "I believe in the holy Christian church"

God's thought was this: in this dark world there would be one group of people so aligned with His thinking and so tuned to His grace that a part of heaven itself might be seen on earth like a light-house on a black night.

God's thought was this: He would have a people, redeemed in the precious blood of His Son, drawn unto Himself through the work of the Spirit, and dedicated to the task of the Kingdom, that would contrast with the world of sinful man and be the instrument for the world's final salvation.

And God called this thought the church. God's thought began in eternity, and it was beautiful and good and pure. Now tell me, is this what the church really looks like? Sometimes perhaps, but most of the time, no. The church has in many instances joined herself quite nicely with the world so that you can hardly tell the difference between the two. For many, the church is just another club to join, another group to find community with. It can be a very disturbing thing to say, "I believe in the Christian church" when it acts like this. What can be more upsetting is that *you* are a part of this church. You share in its glory, but you also share in its sin. Ask yourself, "Am I using the church to actually hide from God, rather than to face up to God's call in the Lord Jesus Christ?" Many Christians do try to hide in the church body and to blend in with the worship and activities of the church. They feel that here they are safe from soul-searching questions by Jesus, "Do you really love Me? Is your life lived in the Spirit of God? Are you losing your life for My sake?"

It is with realization of the church's weakness that you sing each Sunday in the liturgy, "Lord, have mercy." For certainly the church will not be saved by works, but by God's grace in Jesus Christ.

And by God's grace the church can be the church as He intended it to be. In spite of its sin it still is the body of Christ on earth. It still is God's chosen instrument for working His design. You are part of this church. Praise and thank God for this and pray that He makes you a true part of the church, helping it to be that which God intended.

Read Ephesians 3:1–13. It speaks of Paul in prison because he took his ministry seriously and preached the Gospel of Jesus Christ. Why are men like Paul thrown into prison? Did you ever think of the number of imprisonments mentioned in the New Testament: John the Baptist, our Lord Jesus Himself, Peter, James, John, and others? Now read Hebrews 11:32–12:2. Why is this reaction of man to God and His messengers so common? Think of China's anti-Christian goal today. Any time men of God have spoken the full truth of God, the world has always revealed itself for what it is—an enemy of God! Maybe it is hard to imagine yourself as a martyr for Christ. Maybe you think this only happens in far-off places like China. The truth is it happens all over. Certainly you have experience times when you were faced with a situation that you could or could not defend the faith that you believe in. A young Christian has to have "spiritual guts" to faithfully speak the full truth of God to his or her friends.

## "I believe in the communion of saints"

These words should be said in the same breath with those concerning the Christian church: "I believe in the holy Christian church—the communion of saints." This gives meaning to the word "church." It says that it is made up of a fellowship of people. But not any kind of people. It is a fellowship of God's people.

First, you must understand what you are confessing when you say, "I believe in the communion of saints." At school you have your own social group. It is made up of a group of kids like yourself. You don't go around saying, "I believe in my group." Yet in all practices you actually do. If your friend has a problem with his or her parents, it suddenly becomes your problem. If your boyfriend or girlfriend needs some help with his or her math assignment, you offer your humble help. You honestly feel at home with this group of people. They are your friends. This is what you are confessing, though not always knowingly, when you say, "I believe in the communion of saints." You are not saying you believe that the church is made of holier people. But you are saying that here is the greatest fellowship on earth. It transcends all man-made social patterns, all nationalities, all races, the living *and* the dead. It binds you to the Lord Jesus Christ with millions of people whom you have never seen. As you look at this mass of people who love the Lord Jesus, you see this "communion of saints" more as a "team of laborers for God." It is the greatest group on earth—and in heaven.

When a member of this fellowship suffers, you suffer. When one has no roof over his or her head or no food for his or her children, you quickly send aid and offer food. When some of this great fellowship is being persecuted by atheistic governments, you bring this injustice before God. When one is successful in the Father's business, you find yourself suddenly happy. If you traveled anywhere in the world and worshiped with other Christians, you would feel at home in the common words of the Lord. For this fellowship is the great family of God.

Just to say these words, "I believe in the communion of saints," strengthens your faith for the work of the Lord. In this fellowship there are so many, and you by God's grace are one of them.

# Reflections

Look up the following verses and see how they can contribute to your understanding of the word "fellowship."

## Fellowship has . . .

| | |
|---|---|
| —only one entrance | 1 Corinthians 1:9 |
| —strict demand | 2 Corinthians 6:14 |
| —friendship | Galatians 2:9 |
| —loyalty and faithfulness | Ephesians 5 |
| —joy | Philippians 1:3–5 |
| —height and breadth | Romans 8:39 |
| —life | 1 John 1:7 |

This word "fellowship" is from the same Greek word that we translate "communion." See 1 Corinthians 10:16–17. Therefore the "communion" we have with the Lord Jesus in the holy sacrament is also the "communion" we should have with one another.

For your meditation read 1 Corinthians 12:4–30. This is one of Paul's fine passages on the function of the church—the communion of saints. Like a machine composed of many pieces doing many different jobs for a common purpose, the body of Christ is composed of many individuals across time and space doing many different tasks for the common good of the Gospel. In verses 4–11 we see that every Christian has a particular gift or talent that is given him by the Holy Spirit. In verses 12 and 13 we see that even though there are dozens, hundreds, or millions in this grand fellowship, yet it is "one body," called, enlightened, sanctified, and kept by the same Spirit. In verses 14–26 we see that every believer is important, no matter how few or small his talents, because every member of the church is dependent on every other member for the purpose of the church. In verses 27–30, Paul tells us to recognize one another's differences and gifts for the common good of God. God's well oiled machine, His communion of saints work together for the purpose of spreading the Gospel.

## "I believe in the forgiveness of sins"

Few phrases of the creed are said with as much joy as these words: "I believe in the forgiveness of sins." In the forgiveness of sins begins the true fear and love of God.

The forgiveness of sins is the master key that can open up any door in God's Word because it opens up the heart of God. Filled with the Holy Spirit, Zechariah prophesied that his son, John, would "give His people the knowledge of salvation through the forgiveness of their sins" (Luke 1:77). Today we are led to think that the salvation of our world lies in education, money, or international power. All contribute much to man's welfare, but none have the power of salvation. Salvation for any man is in the forgiveness of sins.

This is why God revealed His love for us in the cross of His Son. Here God said to the world, "I forgive you all your sins." A strange place to find salvation, many say. A foolish way, say others. But it's the only place, says God. You cannot get close to God without first understanding the full meaning of the forgiveness of sins.

The forgiveness of sins is very costly. Some Christians think that the forgiveness of sins is an easy pardon handed out upon request by the Almighty God. You hear some say, "All you have to do is to simply ask God for forgiveness." They make God's forgiveness cheap.

To believe in the forgiveness of sins means that you have realized that you are a sinner and that you deserve God's wrath. It means also that with a grateful heart you see the forgiveness of sins that Jesus earned for you. You will then know that such forgiveness is a costly gift. It cost Him everything—it cost Christ His life. And it will cost anybody who seeks the forgiveness of sins everything, too. There is no such thing as receiving the forgiveness of sins and going your own way again. This is the rejection of God's gift He gives you. The forgiveness of sins is the wonderful call of Jesus Christ to follow Him. To follow Jesus is costly because it demands that we give up all sin and condemn all sin. It is God's wonderful gift because it gives a human the only true life—life in Christ. Forgiveness of sins washes us from the stain of sin, placing the sin far away from God's sight, so that the Father sees us through the perfect filter of Christ.

This means that to forgive sins requires divine help. It was not easy for God to forgive. The cross tells us this. For God to forgive you, He had to take your sin with its hurt and agony upon Himself. Christ had to take on the sinful form of humankind to come to earth to bear our sins. Christ took the pain of the diseased, the sorrow of the guilty to forgive the sinful. An example of this type of love that takes on the pain of others can be seen in the movie *The Green Mile*. In this movie the main character John Coffey plays a man on death row. What is most interesting about the movie is the director's choice to make him parallel Christ as he takes on the pain of others. He heals others by taking in their disease. In a similar way, Jesus took on our disease of sin. Jesus bore the weight of each of our sins and the payment of the sin—death—for us! As we forgive each other here on earth, we take the sin of the one who has offended us or our loved ones and bear its hurt and malice willingly and lovingly.

## Reflections

Study 1 John 1–2:17. Be honest with yourself before God as you read this first section of First John. Notice that you cannot speak about the forgiveness of sins that you have received freely from God in Jesus Christ without having the same free forgiveness toward any man who sins against you. Nor can you forgive the sins of your fellow men toward you unless you first experience the forgiveness of God.

Read Psalm 51. To read it with new meaning, get on your knees, then begin slowly. Read one verse at a time, then close your eyes and take this verse to your heart. David wrote this famous psalm after his hideous sin with Bathsheba. This sin could have been David's final downfall. But because he believed in the forgiveness of sins fully and honestly, he was a "man after God's own heart." Note the verbs that are used: "wash . . . cleanse . . . teach . . . purge . . . fill . . . hide." Each verb speaks of God's way of forgiving. Verses 10–12 are customarily sung as the offertory after the sermon. The forgiving God can give you a clean heart and a steady, unwavering spirit. He can give you His Holy Spirit, who will guarantee your salvation and will give you the spirit to serve God and man willingly.

## "I believe in the resurrection of the body and the life everlasting"

There is probably no one word in the language of men that says more than the word "life." Life is everything. Without life everything else is valueless. "Life" can also be the word to sum up the Gospel of Jesus Christ, as the apostle writes, "He who has the Son has *life*." Therefore "life" becomes the concluding and final word in the creed of the Christian Church.

There is a beautiful relationship between the fact of the "resurrection of the body" and the "life everlasting." It reveals this, that everything God has made, He made not just for time, but for eternity. First, let us think on our resurrection. In the beginning, when God created heaven and earth, He saw this creation and said it was very good. It was man, however, His chief creature, who brought His creation under the bondage of sin. Yet in spite of man, God took on his flesh and form so that He could reconcile him back to Himself again. In the fact of man's redemption in Jesus Christ, creation again has hope for the glorious liberty of the children of God. All of this will be seen on the Last Day, when God will raise up you and all the dead and give unto you and all believers in Christ eternal life.

The day of the great resurrection will also be the day of final restoration. Not just the restoration of the "soul" or the "spirit" of man, but the restoration of the physical and material as well. When God makes things new, He makes *all things* new, even your *body*. Therefore you rightly confess, I believe in the "resurrection of the *body*."

That God has made us for eternity is a truth beyond our comprehension. We cannot fathom what eternity is because we are bound by the dimensions of time and space. Eternal life is a continual walking with Jesus. It is the end result of our faith and hope. Therefore the danger of being overly fond of the things of this world lies in the possibility of failing to believe in "life everlasting."

Have you ever wondered what it was like to climb a tall mountain thousands of feet high, and then to stand on the very top and look down all around you? Everything takes on a new perspective. Things you thought big and important don't look that way anymore. As you look out, a whole new horizon can be seen. The creed ends on a mountaintop. From this point you see everything in a more accurate relationship. You get the breathtaking view of the timeless kingdom of heaven. You confess, "I believe in life everlasting."

# Reflections

Read 1 Corinthians 15:20–58. Few chapters in the Scriptures give us a more complete understanding of the resurrection than this one. Its chief thought is this: we have the victory over death through our Lord Jesus Christ. In verses 20–28, we see that the resurrection of all men rests in the resurrection of Jesus Christ. His resurrection was a

→

preview of what is to come (verse 20). You cannot speak about eternal life without also speaking about the resurrection, and vice versa (verses 21–22). In verses 35–50, Paul uses parallels from nature to help us grasp the truths of the resurrection. Paul's use of nature helps us to realize the grandness of the resurrection of the body, but at the same time shows us that it actually cannot be fully explained. In verses 51–58 we have the victory song of heaven. We need people today to know it, believe it, and sing it.

Think about the following references from the Gospel of John. John often speaks of "eternal life." But this is for him both a future and present reality. See 20:31, "you may have life in His name"; 3:16, "but have eternal life"; 10:10, "may have life." Eternal life is what the Christian has now. It is also something for which he or she looks forward to in the future. See 4:14 and note that life begins in a person when he or she believes in Jesus Christ. This life continues eternally. See 5:24 and note the words, "but has crossed over from death to life." John does not say, "will cross," but that a person possesses the life of God at the time he or she comes to faith in Jesus. This explains the apparent contradiction in 11:25, when Jesus says, "he who believes in Me will live, even though he dies." Jesus speaks two truths in the same breath. Young Christian, rejoice that you know Jesus Christ as your Lord and Savior. For since you belong to Him and He to you, you know that you have *life* which is eternal.

Reflections on

# HOLY
# BaptisM

## "Baptism is not just plain water . . ."

Like most Christians, you probably give little if any thought to your Baptism. This is not strange, for most are baptized as little children. It is a heavenly blessing for a child to be brought to the baptismal font and receive this spiritual washing. God had a holy purpose here. But because so many are baptized as small children, they can forget the full meaning of this sacred act. If you were baptized as an adult, you have a distinct advantage. You have the advantage of remembering the great event of this washing of regeneration.

Because our Baptism is something far in the distant past, we say, "Yes, I *was* baptized." This terminology is not helpful. A better way to say this is, "Yes, I *am* baptized." Baptism is a covenant with God that occurs in the present tense, not the past. Your Baptism is not something that has happened and is over with, but it is something that has happened and is still happening.

You don't answer somebody questioning your citizenship, "Yes, I *was* a citizen of the United States." You say, "I *am* a citizen." For those born in the United States your birth gave you the natural right to this citizenship. It happened long ago. You don't recall the event, but because it happened, you are right now a citizen, and you are thankful to God that this great blessing is yours.

You have to be told and taught about your natural citizenship. In school you study history, social studies, and so on. If nobody ever helped you remember your rights and position as a citizen of this country, you never would know that you are a citizen.

If nobody told or taught you about your Baptism, you would not know your rights and privileges of this covenant with God. On the day you received this heavenly washing you were made a citizen of heaven. The Holy Spirit gave you your new papers testifying that you belonged to heaven itself. Through Holy Baptism you now have a position in the Kingdom—today. To a teenager, death seems far-off, something that happens when you are old. This is a problem. Just as death seems far from you now, so your need for baptism seems less than pressing. Any newscast or paper will tell you the staggering number of teen deaths. This is not meant to scare you, but to remind you that death can strike anyone, anytime, at any age. Because of your mortal state, your Baptism becomes critically important to you. Death, the effect of sin, reminds us of our need for a cure—Christ. He has provided the cleansing we need in Baptism. Grow in the full knowledge of your Baptism. Speak about it in the present tense, because you *are* a citizen of heaven.

# Reflections

Read John 3:1–15. This part of John's Gospel deals with the "new birth." Jesus says it is a "must" for any man to enter the kingdom of heaven (verse 7). As you reflect on this familiar discourse of Jesus, think on this illustration. Water seeks its own level. It can rise no higher than its own source. This is a law of nature. This natural law can be applied to spiritual things. If a person starts with him or her self, he or she can rise no higher than self, or we might say the human kingdom. Try as we might, we are only sinful. We cannot rise to the occasion which God sets before us. If we are to save ourselves, we must be perfect. This means perfect in our thoughts and actions and perfect in our nature. As you well know we have a stained human nature, we were

→

born into sin, "Surely I was sinful at birth, sinful from the time my mother conceived me" (Psalm 51:5). And when you look at your own life, you can see your thoughts and actions are sinful. The bar God has set for us is too high. We are not able to jump high enough, do enough good, think lovingly enough, or be faithful enough to gain our own salvation. But to come up to the kingdom of heaven, you must have a source as high, and this source is God Himself. God is the only Source of life. Seeing our sin shows us our need for a savior. Can you better understand Jesus' words, "That which is born of the flesh is flesh, and that which is born of the Spirit is spirit"? We need forgiveness and new life with God! This process of a "new birth" necessary for the new life of God comes through the Holy Spirit and Baptism (John 3:5). As you read this section of John, realize the absolute necessity of the new birth. There are two realms. One is the realm of humans, the other the realm of God. The one is of sin, death, and immorality; the other of life, goodness, and truth. That which is born of each remains and must remain within the area of that which has begotten it or given it birth. No friend of yours will come into the kingdom of God unless he is born again by the Spirit! Think on this! Give God thanks that you have been born the second time through the Sacrament of Holy Baptism and by faith given you by the Spirit of God.

Read Philippians 3:17–21 and Hebrews 11:13–16. By your Baptism and because of your faith in Jesus Christ, you are a citizen of another realm! You belong to an age yet to be revealed. Ask yourself if you are so attached to the things of earth that you may not have the desire to await your Savior, Jesus Christ. The men and women of faith always thought of

$\rightarrow$

the "now" as temporary. Heaven was home. This hope does not take you into some flighty cloud-filled fantasy world; rather it makes you perform your life's vocation with more seriousness. Look forward! God is not ashamed to be called your God.

## "Baptism gives eternal salvation to all who believe this"

Certainly our Lord had children in mind when He instituted Baptism. He was thinking of the Christian family. Baptism is a most precious gift! We think of Peter's remark that Baptism is for "you and your children." Baptism is for every man, woman, and child. It is a "must" for any human being if he or she would enter into the kingdom of heaven. Baptism has a very special blessing for the Christian family as we, God's children, are united together in Him.

We think of a family as the result of sex and social custom. When a man and woman have children, the children are the flesh of their flesh and the blood of their blood. We even say the boy looks like his daddy or the girl has her mother's eyes. Children are the physical offspring of a father and a mother. This is what we think about when we think of a family.

God has far more in mind than simply this. He thinks that the family is the place not just for physical reproduction, where physical life is passed on from one generation to another. A family consists of more than shared genetic traits. A family's love—selfless love and sacrifice—is the relationship God wants with you. You are His child. He is your loving parent, who sacrificed His Son for your life. Just as a parent sacrifices for his or her child, so is God's love shown to us.

God uses the wonderful institution of the family as His method of sharing His life. If a family just passes on physical life, children that are merely born of flesh and blood, they cannot and will not enter the kingdom of heaven. They cannot have the life of God. Only those who are born the second time by water and the Spirit can enter the kingdom. In other words, God demands two births: one is physical, the second is spiritual.

Many years from now, when you get married and have the blessing of bringing children into the world, you have the precious responsibility and blessing to bring your children into the kingdom of God. As you look at your little child, you see in him or her a soul "once born" by you and your spouse. A Christian parent will want to give his or her child the blessing of a "second birth" by bringing the child to the holy font, and there have the saving water poured over the child's head in the name of the Father and of the Son and of the Holy Spirit. Through Baptism you become parents not just in a physical sense, but also in a spiritual sense, passing on God's life to your own.

Here is the joy of the Christian Baptism: that you become a child of God.

## Reflections

Study two short verses of St. John's Gospel, 1:12–13. According to this passage we are the children of God because Christ "gave [us] the right to become the children of God." Like the birthright of the Old Testament, we get God's inheritance—heaven!

→

**Children of God are therefore people:**

—who receive Him, i.e., Jesus

—who believe on His name, i.e., the name of Jesus

—who are born of God

St. John's purpose here is obviously to rule out the thought that the children of God have become the children of God by human works. Only God is able to create children of God! He does this through regeneration (see John 3:5–6). Therefore if you or your children are to become children of God, it is through the creative power and the gracious will of God.

**Thus we are the children of God because we were born:**

| **NOT** | **BY** |
|---|---|
| • of blood (genealogy) | • the blood (of Jesus) |
| • of the will of man | • God |
| • as a result of any cause in man | • the creative power of God |
| • because we were born into a church family | • the Holy Spirit through Baptism |

*but rather …*

Study the following portions of Scripture to better understand that the human family is part of God's design. See the following great beginnings as examples of what God can do with families who surrender to His will and know His grace in Jesus Christ.

*—God began creation with the family—Adam and Eve.*

**See Genesis 1:26–28 and Matthew 19:4.**

What was God's chief purpose in the family?

*—God began a new world with Noah and his family.*

**Skim Genesis 6, 7, and 8.**

Note the unity of this family in their faith in God's Word despite constant ridicule.

*—God began a new people of His own with Abraham and Sarah.*

**See Genesis 12:3; 15:1 and following; 21:1 and following.**

Note that the love and obedience between son and father is exceeded only by their love and obedience to the Lord! (Genesis 22).

*—God began a new nation through families of faith.*

**Skim Exodus 2, 11, 12.**

The importance of the family is very apparent.

*—God began the Promised Land with families of faith.*

**See Joshua 24:15.**

These pioneering families for the Lord are high examples for us and our families in this day and age.

*—God began and fulfilled all things for our salvation in His Son, whom He sent into a human family and subjected to human parents.*

**See Matthew 1 and Luke 1 and 2.**

In Jesus Christ, God reconciled us back into His heavenly family again so that we can be part of His eternal plan for salvation.

*—God began His church with families.*

**See Acts 2:46, 5:42, Colossians 3:18 and following.**

The strength of the church depends still on the strength of the families of the church.

*—God begins a new record with you and your family!*

**See Ephesians 5:21 and following.**

## "It indicates that the Old Adam in us should . . . be drowned and die"

Baptism is a beginning. It is the greatest beginning that you ever experienced and it is not a one time experience. It happens daily! It can be the joyous beginning for the start of each day. You cannot get out of bed in the morning without realizing consciously or unconsciously that you are alive, that you have been born, and that you are in the world of men. God wants you to begin each day by realizing that you are eternally alive through your faith in Jesus

Christ; that you have been born again by the washing of your Baptism and by the power of the Holy Spirit. God wants you to begin each day thinking about that grand beginning.

God has a reason. He wants you to be as clean as on the day of your rebirth through Holy Baptism. He wants you to be as fresh and alive as on the day of His spiritual washing. He wants the power of His risen Son to be working through you all day long. That is why Martin Luther wrote that Baptism "signifies that the old Adam in us should, by daily contrition and repentance, be drowned and die with all sins . . . and a new man daily emerge . . . [to] live before God."

This fact of Baptism which we call daily repentance can be a painful process. Of course, it didn't hurt when water was poured over your head and the pastor pronounced your given name in the saving name of Jesus. But birth of any kind, natural or heavenly, can be painful. Any mother understands the pain of childbirth. So Baptism becomes a painful process of the new birth every time you must drown the old Adam.

A teacher asked his children to define the word "repentance." One little girl defined it this way: "Repentance is when you are sorry enough to quit!" Most of us are sorry over our sins, our evil desires, our tattling tongue, our hates, our prejudices, but not always sorry enough to quit doing and saying and thinking them. In Baptism St. Paul tells us that we are actually buried with Christ. And being buried with Christ means that we must crucify our favorite sins with Him. Any form of crucifixion is a painful experience. It takes all the faith that God can give to us.

If our Baptism is to have everyday significance for us, it means real spiritual sweat on our part. It demands an unwavering heart and a steady mind to live in the new beginning of our heavenly washing. But because it is a beginning each day with Jesus, it is exciting and challenging. It is the greatest beginning that you can experience.

# Reflections

Read Ephesians 4:17–32. As you read, notice the words "put off" (verse 22) and "put on" (verse 24). St. Paul writes in Galatians 3:27, "For all of you who were baptized into Christ clothed yourself with Christ." To cloth yourself with Christ means that we first must take off everything that is not Christ. If you were going to be on TV you would want to come to the studio dressed in a new outfit. When we come before God, we want to present ourselves, pure and clean, in a "new outfit." Paul develops his point that you cannot just put off the old nature, but that you must put on the new nature (verses 25 and following). Perhaps the following table will help you see Paul's thought:

## Putting Off Your Old Nature

**It is not enough just to stop:**

- *falsehood (verse 25)*
- *sinful anger (verse 26)*
- *any form of stealing (verse 28)*
- *unwholesome talk (verse 29)*
- *bitterness, anger, and any form of unkindness (verses 31–32)*

→

## Putting On the New Nature

**But begin to:**

- *speak the truth (verse 24)*
- *master your temper (verse 24)*
- *work with the talents God has given you (verse 24)*

Now think through your results. Do you follow Paul's thought? Pray about this.

Read Romans 6:1–23. The accusation is made against those who confess God's grace in order to live in sin. This idea of the lazy or corrupt Christian who can sin as often as he or she feels like it is wrong. Perhaps you have given people this idea too. Perhaps you think that you can sin—just once—with the reservation that God forgives. Such a thought runs contrary to the entire idea of God's grace and the purpose of your eternal, blood-bought salvation. The purpose of God's grace in Jesus Christ is to free you from sin so that you no longer sin but live a holy and perfect life before God and humanity. With this thought in mind, read chapter six of Romans, and find the power for the new life in Jesus Christ.

Reflections on

# HoLY
# CoMMunioN

## "It is the true body and blood of our Lord . . ."

Some believe that the Holy Communion instituted by our Lord is a mere tradition in the church. Some feel that it is something that you can take or leave with little loss or gain either way. Such thinking is not only wrong, it is close to blasphemy. For the Sacrament of Holy Communion is God's special way of communicating His life, His forgiveness, His peace, His power to you. For the world He gave the Gospel, for He would have all men to be saved and come to the knowledge of the truth. But for His church He gave the Sacrament of Holy Communion. When God comes to us in the sacrament, it cannot be labeled "tradition," but it must be called what it is, a "holy, very holy, communion."

Phillips in his *Appointment with God* compares the sacrament to a pipeline running unbroken through all the church's history right back to Jesus Christ Himself. This is a good picture. It shows us how Jesus wants to come all the way to us right where we are. He comes to us who have life's problems and cares. So many times our thinking is in reverse. We think *back* to Jesus. When we study about Him or talk about Him, so many times we think of something 2,000 years ago, rather than looking forward into our life today. We talk about the cross and the open tomb as has-beens, saying, "Look how wonderful. This is what happened then." But in the Sacrament of Holy Communion we can say, "This is what is happening now." The sacrament takes that first Good Friday and moves it right into our own century, for Jesus says, "Take, eat; this is My body, which is given for you." The sacrament takes that first Easter and transfers its power and its life right into us today.

Jesus is no longer far away. He is no longer so high up that He becomes unreal to us. He is no longer just a figure in history who cannot help us. But in the sacrament Jesus is *here:* Jesus Christ who died for our sins and rose again for our justification—this Jesus— this same Jesus! The real presence of our Lord in the holy sacrament should encourage us to partake of Communion as often as it is celebrated by our congregation. For at the Table Jesus Himself has us eat and drink His true body and blood, which is in, with, and under the bread and the wine. Truly, He comes all the way to His church.

# Reflections

Read 1 Corinthians 11:23–29. This is Paul's account of the institution and meaning of Holy Communion. Luther called the sacrament the "visible Word." It summarizes and visualizes the Gospel for us. Read this section and see how it speaks of our Lord's incarnation, i.e., He became flesh and dwelt among us, His atoning and redeeming death for sin on the cross, His glorious resurrection, His second coming for judgment, His life and salvation, and His judgment on unbelief. The sacrament not only preaches Christ but gives us Christ's body and blood as well.

In preparation for receiving the holy Sacrament of the Altar think about Psalm 32. This is called a penitential psalm. It was written by David, who was one man who understood the forgiveness of sins. David speaks of a person who is truly happy and content as one who has the forgiveness of sins. This does not mean the person who just knows about

→

the forgiveness of sins, but the person who lives in the forgiveness of sins. Guilt and remorse are the two greatest factors in mental breakdown and emotional distress today. We are living in a world that does not know the forgiveness of sins. David confesses that at one time he did not think it necessary to confess his sins to God (32:3–4). If you have a sin and do not confess it to God, or in private confession to your pastor, or to the party whom you wronged, your everyday life can be a hell on earth. Your nights will be filled with restless sleep. Yet this is what millions go through every day and every night. David learned this lesson—David did confess his sins and was forgiven. And where there is forgiveness of sins, there is life (verses 5 and following). Where there is forgiveness of sins, there is God's guidance and protection in every walk of life (32:8–9). Where there is forgiveness of sins, there is really joy (verse 11). **Whenever you eat this bread and drink this cup, you proclaim the Lord's death until He comes again. I Corinthians 11:26**

We can become very attached to our little earth. We become attached to our cars, our clothing, our homes, our many pleasures, our material things. We like this world and everything in it so much that at times we really have no desire for the new world. Men and women of faith have always wrestled with this tension, yet have come up with the bold cry: "This world is not our home; we wait for the world to come." In faith they looked for something bigger and better. In faith this is also our blessed condition, that as citizens of another country we live as foreigners on earth.

Dr. Martin Luther makes much of this. He repeats time and again that the Christian is like the man who comes to the inn for the night. He has no thought of staying there forever. But he knows that on the next day or in the near future he will move on. The inn provides a place for his rest. But it never becomes his sole house and home.

This was so true of our Lord Jesus. All during His earthly life He recognized that His citizenship in His Father's country remained unimpaired and that His residence for thirty-three years among men did not naturalize Him as a citizen of earth. Scripture calls Jesus' earthly ministry a "visit." All the time He was among men He remained a citizen of heaven.

You must keep this in mind as you prepare for the holy sacrament. For you are not like the man who stands on earth and looks up to heaven, but rather like the man who is in heaven and looks down upon earth. The holy sacrament helps you put everything into a new view and gives life a new set of horizons.

Jesus knew that you would be overly attracted to your car and clothing and all the things of earth. Jesus knows you well. That is why He desires you to partake of that food from heaven. It is food that this world knows nothing about and cares less. But Jesus said, "I am the Bread of Life which came down from heaven." Thus in the sacrament you receive spiritual nourishment of the "other" country.

A young married couple living on the West Coast had a father on the East Coast who was a well-known baker. They always rejoiced when they received a box of his special rye bread still fresh from his ovens. The young bride said, "It is a taste of home." Exactly! How we should love to receive under bread and wine the very body and blood of Jesus, the Bread of Life. It is a taste of home!

# Reflections

Read John 6. This chapter has been named the "Bread of Life" chapter. As you read, note the development of unbelief and belief. The more Jesus reveals Himself as the true Bread from heaven, the more the unbelief of many of the people is revealed, and the more the belief of some, i. e., the twelve, is recognized (6:66–69). Study carefully the following misunderstandings of the Jews, which are the same today as then.

## Misunderstandings

—*political aspirations of Judaism (verse 15)*

—*the gift from Jesus of bread and fish (verses 26–27)*

—*the Scriptural story of Moses and their fathers (verses 32, 49–51)*

—*truth (verses 35–41)*

—*Life (verses 51–52)*

—*the necessity of Jesus' words concerning His flesh and blood and the nature of His mission (verses 53 and following)*

→

Pray that you have none of these misunderstandings, but firmly believe that Jesus is the Bread of Life and that His body and blood were given and shed for you on the cross for your salvation from sin, death, and hell.

Before coming to Holy Communion think about Psalm 103. Notice three things. First, who the Lord is and what He does. Second, notice how the Lord forgives sins. Do you forgive others the way God forgives? (103:10–12). Third, notice how the earthly life of man is compared to the eternal life of God's love (103:15–18). And finally in verses 19–22 the psalmist sings to every part of God's creation, including his own soul, to wake up and bless the Lord God.

## "The words 'for you' require all hearts to believe"

So many times we can miss Jesus. We come to church for worship, and what happens? We do everything but worship our Lord. We don't come to Him, and we cleverly close our ears and eyes so that we prohibit Him from coming to us. We sit down in the pew taking notice of who is or isn't in church this particular Sunday. Then the opening hymn begins, but our mind is on last night's date, and all the wonderful words sung about Jesus don't reach our flighty brains. The pastor reads the Scriptures, words of life written by men of the Spirit, words of love spoken by Jesus Himself, but we are looking at the funny hat on the lady three pews ahead or wondering if Mr. Smith will ever get another suit. During the sermon we dutifully look up at the preacher, but actually we look right through him into next week's schedule of schoolwork and sports practices, and that problem we had with that friend. You see, Jesus wanted to visit with you so very much, but you didn't permit Him.

Then comes the Sacrament of the Altar. No matter how you have avoided Jesus up to this point, you can avoid Him no further. You have to kneel before Him, and getting down before the altar tells you that He is your Master and you are only His servant. Then comes the bread and the wine. You can't daydream anymore. You have to begin to think about what you are doing. Jesus is saying to you, "You can't miss Me anymore, friend. The devil thought he had won the day. But at last you must really look at Me and think of what I did for you. You can't miss Me here—take and eat—take and drink."

With the bread and the wine you are truly eating and drinking Christ's body and blood. At the same time Jesus says to you, "Your sins are forgiven." And they are! Jesus has visited you in a supernatural manner. You can't forget Him after this. You go back to your pew, and you look up at the cross and realize what a wonderful Lord and Savior you have. He loves you very much. He knows you too well. He wants to visit with you continually in His Word and Sacrament. Then you bow your head for a prayer of real thanksgiving.

# Reflections

To think about Holy Communion, read Psalm 130. The soul of the psalmist feels the true weight of sin; the mind of the psalmist comprehends the burden of iniquity. You cannot understand the psalms by merely studying them. Even all the knowledge of Hebrew could not lead you into the full meaning. Only when you experience the condition that the psalmist feels in his heart, can you begin to apprehend the full impact of his message. Thus if you have never been in the "depths," you will fail to comprehend his crying to the Lord. The key verses are 3 and 4. Here the psalmist asks a very good question. Ask yourself this question. What answer do you get? Verse 4 is the key to understand Dr. Martin Luther's words of his *Small Catechism,* "We should fear and love God." The fear and the love for God comes only to the man who has experienced the forgiveness of sins! The word "fear" does not mean being scared of. Rather it means standing in awe of God.

Read Luke 8:40–56. Few accounts of Jesus' healing are more touching than these. But they are more than just touching. They tell us that every individual is important to Jesus. If you come to Him in prayer, you will not get away unnoticed. See the little girl as twelve years of laughter and life. See the woman with her twelve years of sorrow and sickness. Twelve years of bitterness in contrast with twelve years of joy suddenly ended in death. Then comes Jesus. He deals with each one individually. This is what Jesus does and can do for you in the holy sacrament. No matter who you are or what your problem may be, when you come to Him, you cannot go away unhealed.

Reflections on

# THe Ten CoMMaNDments

## "We should fear and love God"

I have always associated dating with the First Commandment. You don't like to go on a date with somebody who doesn't want to go on a date with you. You want to date someone who is very interested in you and wants to be with you. This is what God wants too. He doesn't want people to go along with Him because they have to. He wants people to go along with Him because they want to. He wants people freely to do those good things and think those good thoughts that are in accordance with His holy will and glorify His name. Yet, you and I both know we do not do those things nor are we capable of doing them.

We are not capable? Try as we will, we continually find ourselves failing before God's Law. "Have no other gods." It sounds simple enough. I haven't found a golden calf to worship, nor do I want to. But gods can come in all forms—money, friends, popularity. Then there are the other nine. I try Lord, but why can't I keep them? We can't keep the Law of the Lord because we are humans whose very nature is sinful. Try as we might, we always find ourselves failing in comparison to the perfect Law of God—the Law that expects perfection. This is one of the purposes of the Law, to show us our sin. With the perfect rule of God there before us, we are reminded of our need for a Savior. The Law shows us that before God we are incapable and need His help.

This is why God sent Jesus to redeem us. Jesus redeemed us by His suffering, death, and resurrection, not just that we may gain heaven, but that God would have a "new" people. New people for God are those who have been born through Holy Baptism. These new people do not have to be commanded and coerced in their actions, thoughts, and words, but they are people who cheerfully do, think, and speak as God's will directs them. This may seem to be a description of heaven, but it also is a description of what God wants to begin to happen to us on earth. God wants us to be so alive with the life of Jesus that we will be performing the will of the Father even as Jesus did.

But it doesn't always work out this way. We find ourselves really struggling in the faith. The reason is simple—the devil doesn't want to let you go. And the more you grow in the Lord Jesus, the more you realize this tension. For we do those things we know we shouldn't do and don't do those things we know we should.

Here is where the Ten Commandments can be a guide for us. Understand there is no life in the commandments. All they can do is help you understand what you are doing wrong and what you should be doing right. The commandments are like the speed laws posted in your town. They may say 35 MPH. But this does not mean that everybody goes 35 MPH. Laws—even God's—don't make people good. Laws show us that we are not good. They may even, by instilling fear, compel external compliance with them. But they have no life-power. Life-power comes only in the Good News of Jesus Christ.

You want to pray for this life-power. The power of the resurrected Christ is your power by faith. In Him you can actually begin doing things for God because you just want to. You will have the eyes of faith to see what should be done, and you will have the power of the Spirit to actually do them.

Here is perfect freedom! Freedom from sin and from the Law to serve God willingly. Christ has made you free. Stand fast in your freedom.

# Reflections

Study Ephesians 2:1–10. God had a real purpose in redeeming us from sin and death. His purpose was to have a people who would serve Him willingly and do those things that are pleasing to Him. See verses 8 and 9. They are one of the finest statements on the fact that a man can be saved solely by God's grace and not by his merits or works. But too often this beautiful passage is memorized out of context. Let us see the relationship of verses 8 and 9 with verses 1–10. Underline the verb "walk" in both verses 2 and 10. This little word "walk" is used in two settings, each contrary to the other. Note the two paths referred to in verse 2 and in verse 10. One is the path of sin prepared by Satan, the other the path of goodness prepared by God. The former path is the one you "once walked;" the latter is the one in which you "should walk." Now God's grace in Jesus Christ has saved you from the path of sin for the path of goodness. When you believe in the Lord Jesus Christ and understand His free gift of salvation and forgiveness, then you want to be doing those good works that please God and benefit your fellow man.

Read Exodus 20:1–20. This is the first account in the Bible of the giving of the Ten Commandments. It is a moving and dramatic scene. But it is more than dramatic. Few take God's Law seriously today. But God takes His Law seriously even as He takes man's sin seriously. God was not being dramatic with the thunder and lightning or the shaking mountain. This was the holy, righteous Almighty One of heaven confronting sinful man. The encounter was one of Law, therefore of judgment. Therefore nature quakes, and any man will die if he sets foot on this holy place of God. There is no life in the Law, yet people continually say, if you keep the Ten Commandments, you shall go to heaven. The pity with this group is they never have been to Mount Sinai. Yet we esteem God's Law because it is good. It directs us who believe and who are saved from sin and death to perform God's will on earth.

## "If the Lord is God, follow Him; but if Baal, follow him" (1 Kings 18:21).

The young man asked, "Pastor, can I go on a date with this girl I met this coming Saturday night?" The pastor answered, "I don't know. Can *you*?"

This was not exactly what Shawn expected. He was hoping that the pastor would either condone his going or give him a reason to tell this girl why he could not. He was afraid to make his own decision. This young man never thought the entire matter through for himself. He did not realize the Christ-won freedom he possessed, nor did he understand the personal responsibility of making a Spirit-guided decision in this matter.

We always talk about "freedom," but too often we are afraid to assume the tasks and responsibilities of our freedom. St. Paul emphasizes over and over again that Christ has made you free. He meant every word that he said. You are free to make your own decision in ethical matters. The church can give counsel. The pastor can give direction. Parents can give advice. All should be taken seriously and respectfully. But you must make the decision. Your decision must be aligned with the will of your heavenly Father. It must be carried out in the power of the Holy Spirit.

You cannot escape from decisions. Even if you don't like this fact, you must live a life of unavoidable decisions. And remember, not to make a decision is also a decision—a bad one. You ask, "How can I make God-pleasing decisions? What can help me do the things I should do and prohibit me from doing the things I should not do? . . . I know I shouldn't kill, lie, or commit adultery. God's Law speaks plainly on these matters. But in my everyday life I face harder problems than these; harder, because everybody has a different set of values." You are right. Everybody makes decisions on the basis of different standards. Their standards are their gods. They consciously or unconsciously commit themselves to a certain set of values.

But your commitment should be rather clear. Your commitment is to the Lord Jesus Christ. He becomes the standard for evaluating all your daily decisions. Jesus is the absolute standard for all Christian ethics. As we grow in our faith, the Holy Spirit strengthens us in His Word. God gives us the ability to make the right decisions. The Ten Commandments and their interpretation by Jesus provide a good framework to consider what Jesus expects of you. You can make the right decisions only in a faith that commits you to Christ. Dr. Martin Luther said, "Faith alone makes all other works good, acceptable, and worthy."

Read 1 Kings 18. The Old Testament gives us sharp and clear illustrations concerning man and God. This familiar story of Elijah paints with sharp strokes the unalterable fact that you are either with God or against God. There is no middle ground. Nor will God permit any. Read verse 21. How many times could this prophet of God say these same words to you? You had a big decision to make for truth, but you "did not answer . . . a word." As the rest of this story shows, God will not let you rest in silence; you must give an answer.

## "You shall have no other gods"

The saying goes that "50 million Frenchmen cannot be wrong." Sometimes we believe this. If everybody thinks one way, that one way must be the right way to think. So many people cannot be wrong.

Your best friend tells you her exciting news, somebody, who knew someone, got it. Tonight all of your friends are going to get together. One of them had borrowed a friend's bong and they are going to smoke some marijuana. And you are invited. They, all of your friends, are going to do it. No big deal right? Plus everyone tries it. Everybody does it. Right?

God is unconcerned with the idea that the majority is always right. His Word stands, without question. God saved the seed of human life not with a nation or a tribe or a clan, but with a solitary family, that of Noah, as He flooded out the rest of life. Sodom and Gomorrah perished not because of the vast wicked majority, but because there was no right minority. On Good Friday a solitary figure hung on the cross with the whole world against Him. Look back across the centuries and ask, "Whose was the victory?" Was it with the majority who cried, "Give us Barabbas," or was it with that one Man who said, "Father, forgive them for they do not know what they are doing"? Jesus was only one. When you say, "I will have no other gods before You, O Lord," you are saying that your relationship with God comes before the majority every time. But to say this, you dare have no other commitments, no other masters, no other gods. God has to be All in all in your life. "You shall have no other gods [before Me]!" says your God. If you have this faith, then all good works will follow in their right order.

It may be an uncomfortable question, but sit alone for a time and ask yourself, "What is *my* faith? In *whom* do I really believe?" This is the first thing to answer. If the answer comes out that there are no other gods, no other loves, no other names in addition to that of the Lord Jesus Christ, then you can be sure that He and you will constitute the majority every time.

## Reflections

Read 1 Samuel 17. Do not skim this chapter just because the story of David and Goliath is familiar. Try reading it out loud to grasp the full content of its message. At first glance David seems naive in his faith in God. Yet it is this childlike faith that God is looking for. Listen to Saul, "you are only a

→

boy." Now listen to David, "The Lord ... will deliver me from the hand of this Philistine" (17:33, 37). God does not need an army of Goliaths. God needs more Davids. For David was a young man who had no other gods before the true God. Thus God and he were a majority.

Read Daniel 3. It is one thing to stand up and recite, "You shall have no other gods," but it is quite another to stand before a king on whose hands your life depends and say, "I will not worship the golden image that you have set up." Faith is more than a matter of the lips; it is also a matter of action. And in this case, bold, courageous, daring action. When all the people were bowing down to the false god of Nebuchadnezzar, three young men stood. This is the kind of people God is looking for. When all other young people are bowing down to the god of popularity, the god of sex, and the god of wealth, God's young men and young women will stand and bear witness to the triune God and His Word.

## "You shall not misuse the name of the Lord your God"

We always like to draw attention to ourselves. Whether it is our clothing, our car, our sports record, or our friend group, we naturally seek attention. Whether it is attention from the opposite sex or our friends or even complete strangers, we simply like to draw attention to ourselves. Many of the things we do and many of the things we say as well as many of the decisions we make say just this.

In the Second Commandment God tells us that our lives are supposed to draw attention to the goodness of Jesus rather than to our own alleged goodness. What we say and do should draw attention not to our own name, but to God's name. God says that when we do good works that result from a strong faith in Him, then these good works will be seen by men, and they will glorify Him. Thus the Second Commandment deals with the good name of God.

Most certainly you do not want to misuse *this name*. An older translation of this commandment used the word "vain" for the way people misuse God's name. In this context vain means "empty." If you go about your daily living, and the things you say and decisions you make and things you do are all empty of the Lord Jesus Christ, then you are taking the Lord's name in vain—you are misusing His name. Think of this name—this was the name that was glorified by the atoning sacrifice of the Son of God upon the cross—this was the name that has become your way to heaven—this name is the name above all names. You dare not live a life empty of the name of the Lord Jesus. God will not hold any guiltless who take His name in vain.

The name of the triune God is bound to everything that is true and good. Therefore, do not speak Truth when that truth misuses God's name. We do not speak Truth when we deny justice or fail to hold up the good. Both are ways of misusing God's name. Since by Baptism you are also received into the name of God, your lives dare not be empty of that name, nor of truth, goodness, or justice. You must speak against all wrong and always fight for what is right. You must never permit yourself or your fellow man to take God's name in vain.

The Second Commandment makes us rather uncomfortable. It is supposed to! It wakes us up to our emptiness—that we like to draw attention to self and not to the Lord. It jolts us to see how empty of the Lord Jesus most of our living is. But it also shows us that by faith we can become so identified with the name of our Lord that we can actually draw people to His truth and His goodness.

# Reflections

Read the fourth chapter of Ruth. Remember that to keep the Second Commandment is to keep truth, so that God's name might be glorified. Note three things as you meditate on this familiar story. According to the Law of Moses in Deuteronomy 25:5, when a man died without children, it was the office and duty of the next of kin to marry his widow and raise up a family with the name and rights of her first husband. For this reason, Boaz, a high-standing townsman and relative to Naomi, called a meeting of the city fathers at the "gate." The "gate" was a convenient place to congregate for business and community meetings because it was shaded by the arch. Here Boaz asked the "next of kin" to assume his responsibilities (Ruth 4:1–4). The man (whose name is not given!) refused when he learned he must marry Ruth (Ruth 4:5–6), because Ruth was a foreigner and this might ruin his name. He was more concerned about drawing attention to his good name than drawing attention to God's! He gave up the duty as kinsman and disregarded God's Law because it interfered with his way of living. So Boaz married Ruth, being the next kin in line (Ruth 4:7–12). Boaz thought more of God's Law than of his own name. And Boaz received the everlasting honor of having his name on the first page of the New Testament (see Matthew 1:5), while

→

the first kinsman is lost to memory. Boaz honored God's name by obeying God's Word and therefore kept the Second Commandment.

Read Romans 2:17–24. Paul is speaking to his fellow Jews. In place of the word "Jew" write "Christian." Could Paul write this to young people of the church today? Pray that verse 24 can never be said against you! Rather as Matthew 5:16 discusses, try to be the light of God before others.

## "Remember the Sabbath Day by keeping it holy"

If you have ever had a younger or older sibling of a few years you will understand the idea of worship. As a small child looks up to an older sibling, we say, the child "worships the ground he or she walks on." This conveys a real meaning of "worship." What we mean when we say this is that that child adores everything that older brother or sister does. They want to play with the older sibling, look and act like him or her. The child goes through the day as though nobody else existed except the older brother or sister. This is worship. Because worship means to honor, adore, and esteem. And to worship God means that we honor, adore, and esteem Him above everything else.

Worship is an activity that can never be forced. You can be forced to go to church, but nobody can ever force you to worship. Worship is a spontaneous act. It flows from a heart of faith. It is a result of the life in the Holy Spirit. Worship is the outward evidence that you love the Lord Jesus.

Think again about the little brother or sister that adores the older sibling. The adoration of the child naturally pours out into the behavior of the child. Oftentimes following the older brother or sister around, asking questions, and dressing or imitating the older brother or sister. This natural action of the child is like our natural action or response to God and what He has done for us. When a person says that he or she is a follower of Christ, that he or she honors God above all others, that he or she loves His Word, but fails to gather with other Christians for worship, we would question the reality of this person's faith. For as natural as it is to emulate one you admire, so natural is the worshiping of God for the Christian.

In neglecting or failing to worship God you are saying, "God doesn't love me anymore, and I don't love Him. There is no purpose in our meeting together." God knows better. He knows that we need to worship Him. Worship centers in the new life of the Son of God, who makes all things new because He has redeemed us by His blood. Therefore we hold God's Word sacred and gladly hear and learn it.

## Reflections

Read Revelation 7:9–17. St. John paints a picture of the church in glory worshiping God. Someone has said that worship is one thing that we do on earth that we will be doing in heaven. Therefore it is truly one of the prime tasks for the church on earth. Notice the size of the multitude about the throne (verses 9–12). The whole scene is overwhelming. The beautiful reference to the atoning and

→

redeeming work of our Lord Jesus Christ (verses 13–15) shows the reason for our worship. The picture of heaven goes beyond our greatest imagination. Here we see John trying to express the inexpressible. Certainly we sense the joy of pure praise and the love of true worship.

Read Luke 10:38–42. Some people mistakenly think that Martha's work was somehow more important than Mary listening to Jesus. Some people in your church or youth group will devote much of their time to various church activities but little time to hearing God's Word. These people can fall into a trap of becoming angry with those who put Bible study and church attendance first. Note the word "distracted" in verse 40. Martha was distracted by her work. Her activities took her attention away from the Word. Don't ever become so busy in activities, work, and projects that these things take your attention away from the "one thing [which] is needed" (10:42).

## "Honor your father and your mother"

The Fourth Commandment brings the realm of authority under the dominion of the Gospel of Jesus Christ, for all legitimate authority rests in Jesus. All authority in this world must find its roots in God and His Son and must reveal itself as an opportunity for serving mankind.

Jesus, the ultimate authority, places on the earth two roles of authority. Those in authority to us are our parents and the government. First, *you* are to obey your parents. Jesus knows that you think your parents are very unreasonable at times, that they don't understand *you*, and that they are old-fashioned in their ways. But the command is clear, "Honor your father and your mother." Parents are Jesus' way of taking care of you. Yes, your parents feed and clothe you, but their care extends into the law. This seems cruel. In the caring role of the parent, God places authority. This authority is to curb us from sin. Just as the little child's mother punishes the child who steals a cookie from the jar to keep a bad habit from forming, so does the loving parent curb the teen from temptations. In this way, parents not only care for their children's physical needs, but their spiritual needs as well. Therefore a parent who stops a son from cussing or a daughter from stealing candy loves the child by reprimanding him or her.

The enemies of the Christian faith understand the importance of the Christian family, sometimes better than we do. Many formerly Communist countries tried to replace the Christian family unit with the state government. If parents and children loved each other in the Lord Jesus, they were a dangerous cell of opposition to the efforts of a godless state to become the "mother" or the "father." In the end, many of these countries fell because the families remained strong. The state, the church, or the school can never take the place of the Christian home.

The second area that the Fourth Commandment addresses is government. As a child of God your interest is how His message and His work can be spread here on earth. As a citizen of a government, you have a field to do this work in. This does not mean that you necessarily must become a political activist. Rather this means you attempt to show that the power of the government is ultimately dependent upon God. Jesus is not just the Head of the church, but also Lord of the state, whether or not He is recognized as such.

What this means is that your faith plays out in how you see your world and how you interact with it. Yes, God rules all, even your government, but how does your faith play into your interaction with the world? A Christian can stand up for Christ and His Word in the political realm by knowing God's Word and defending it. A Christian can understand what murder is and support the pro-life movement. A Christian can understand Christian love and charity, and support its efforts in the world. The political realm is more than bills and laws; it is God's decrees played out in reality to real people who need to know Him. Jesus is Lord. And this fact must affect all your relationships in this world. This is essential to the Fourth Commandment.

# Reflections

Read Genesis 22. This story of Abraham and Isaac portrays a God-pleasing example of obedience and love. God's gift of faith allowed Abraham to carry out this act of faith and trust (see Hebrews 11:17–20). Through Abraham, God would carry out His grand design for salvation.

Isaac becomes a picture of Jesus, carrying the wood up the hill on which he would be sacrificed. The climax of the story is in verses 13 and 14, where God provides a ram. This is a true foreshadowing of the Lamb of God slain for our sins. Now this entire story would never have happened if either Abraham or Isaac had not been obedient in their respective callings. God has a design and a method in saying

→

to us, "Obey." Our obedience to our Lord and to those who He has placed over us is a true act of faith.

Read the first chapter of Daniel. If you have time, read the entire book. True, it contains many mysterious prophecies that speak a language of another world. But there is also a down-to-earth truth that you must not overlook. Daniel, a man of God, became a key political figure in both the realm of Nebuchadnezzar and the realm of Darius. Daniel started his brilliant career as a teenager in the courts of Nebuchadnezzar. Daniel was totally obedient to his Lord and to His Word (verses 8–9). The Law commanded what to eat and what not to eat. Daniel's obedience to these laws showed his faith in God as he challenged his earthly king to be obedient to his heavenly one. Obedience demands faith, and God can do big things with men who have such faith. By faith Daniel prevailed, and by faith Daniel showed that the power of any government depends ultimately upon the power of God (see 3:28–30 and 6:25–28). Our country needs people of faith like Daniel. God is looking for young people who are faithful to Him in all things.

## "You shall not murder"

Every time a young child dies because of lack of food or a family perishes because there is no clothing for their bodies or roof over their heads, the world stands judged by God. And this includes you! The holy Law of God holds you as well as everyone accountable for the welfare of people—all people, whoever they are and wherever they might be. You have the joy of taking care of people both in your local community and in the international community. You cannot live in isolation. You cannot have faith in Jesus Christ without having Jesus' love and concern for people—all people. Jesus redeemed you that you might do good works. Good works for Jesus always mean good for other people.

This is what the Fifth Commandment is saying to us. Obviously we do not go around killing people, at least not with a knife or a gun. This seems like an obvious breaking of the Fifth Commandment. But what about the less obvious murders that happen every day? Oftentimes we think of murder only as the shootings we hear about on the six o'clock news. Murder happens in other forms than guns and knives. The Fifth Commandment discusses murders by other names: abortion, euthanasia, and suicide. The world covers this up in a different name, trying to make these types of murders acceptable, but they never are. Be it a baby, the chronically diseased, or terminally ill, when we play God and determine the end of one's life, we have committed a sin.

There is one other less obvious sin against the Fifth Commandment. It is probably the one we do the most often—angry thoughts. John 3:15 says, "Anyone who hates his brother is a murderer, and you know that no murderer has eternal life in him." Thanks be to Christ that you are no longer a murderer, but a forgiven child of God. This gives all of us the reason to share this message with others and in so doing help them in their needs. Dr. Martin Luther rightly understands the meaning of this commandment, saying that we should help and befriend people in their bodily needs. Instead of hating our neighbor, we can love them as our brothers and sisters in Christ, and help them in their physical needs.

Of course, you cannot feed all the hungry in the world, cure all the sick, house all the homeless. Thank God that you have been saved by His grace and not by your works. As Christians, every other person's bodily need becomes our need. Every human ailment becomes our concern. This means giving blood to the blood bank; clothing to world relief; doctors and nurses to the sick and dying; social workers to the needy; Habitat for Humanity projects; contributing to cancer research; participation in law enforcement, and the like. Your love for God develops in you a real, active concern for all people, a concern that drives that you pray for them, love them, and help them.

This is a hard commandment to fulfill. Basically, we are loveless. We are self-centered, not people-centered. But Jesus is Love. His love redeems us from self-love and lets us begin loving people as He did. You can never know real love until you know Jesus. For in Jesus, God shows and gives His kind of love. And His kind of love is the only kind that has a sacrificial and a redemptive concern for all people. Grow in the love of Jesus Christ, your Lord, and you will "Love your enemies and pray for those who persecute you, that you may be the sons of your Father in heaven" (Matthew 5:44–45).

# Reflections

Read 1 John 4:7–21. John shows us that our relationship with God is evident in our relationship with men. Some people misunderstand this relationship. These misunderstandings can work in three different ways. They forget that the basic and most important relationship is faith in the great truths about God and complete trust in God's forgiving love, expressed through Jesus' self-sacrifice. Others for-

→

get that the natural, inevitable fruit of faith is love of God and of all people. According to John you can't have one without the other. John says that you cannot speak about faith in God without having love toward other people. There is a third group that says you can love people and have no need for God's love. They are wrong too. Study verses 7–12 and note that it is "not that we loved God, but that He loved us." The secret to loving people, especially those who you don't like or can't stand, is to allow God's love for you to grow.

Read Matthew 5:21–26 and 38–48. In our cold, cruel world do you think that Jesus' ideas are workable? Can a Christian justify the dropping of a nuclear bomb that will kill millions and injure millions more? Can you become a successful businessman in our "dog-eat-dog" world by always turning the other cheek? At the beginning, Jesus' instructions here seem to make us soft and easygoing. But this is not so. Think through these questions, and discover the true fiber of an individual prepared for the kingdom of God.

## "You shall not commit adultery"

Sex was God's idea. Many people think that humans dreamed it up. But God made sex, for we read, "Male and female He created them" (Genesis 1:27). In His eternal wisdom God dreamed up this physical attraction between the man and the woman. He made sex something very beautiful. Again we read, "God saw all that He had made, and it was very good" (Genesis 1:31a). This includes sex.

Now if sex was God's idea, God must have a purpose in placing this urge in every one of us. It must have been a wonderful idea too. For some people, sex is considered something dirty. It is associated with the unclean and the filthy. Why? The reason is that when humans fell into sin, they degraded and corrupted all the good things that God made and used them for their selfish ends. The gift of sex was one of the highest and most noble gifts. The result, humans have taken this gift and brought it to the lowest and filthiest levels in human relationships. Sex is not sinful; humans are. Therefore only the redeemed, renewed, reborn individual in Jesus Christ actually can use sex for God's original purpose.

God's purpose was this, that two people, male and female, might become one. The union of two people is the purpose of sex. And Jesus said, "For this reason a man will leave his father and mother and be united to his wife, and the two will become one flesh. So they are no longer two, but one. Therefore what God has joined together, let no man separate" (Matthew 19:5–6). Anything that would break up this marriage is hated by God. God hates divorce! It opposes the prime purpose of marriage: united selfless love and children. God also hates any sexual acts that are outside of marriage. Going too far pushes one into the sin of lust. Not only is this a sin against the Sixth Commandment, but against the gift of marriage. Sexual activity outside of marriage lessens the beauty of the united bond God gives when sex is saved for marriage.

Sex is a gift when it is viewed in the love of Jesus. It should never be motivated by lust. Lust merely desires to fulfill the body's physical pleasures. Lust devalues your partner to being an object. You look at that person as an object that can fulfill your needs, not a person you love, and certainly not a child of God. Love is using sex in a God-pleasing manner to show true affection and genuine concern for the welfare and happiness of your lifetime mate. Sex is therefore the ultimate outpouring of a married couple sharing themselves with one another.

We obey the Sixth Commandment, not because of negative reasons. But rather because we actually love our "love" with the love of Jesus. We want to use the precious gift of sex for God's purpose of marriage and the joy of a Christian family.

## Reflections

Read 1 Corinthians 13. This is Paul's famous poem on love. When people get married and have a church wedding, they get caught up in the many details of what must be bought or planned for the day, losing track of the one important detail—God. Often they forget details, important plans like picking a wedding text. Often 1 Corinthians 13 is used as a reading at a wedding. After reading this lovely chapter, let us select the first three verses as a wedding text. How might we apply these verses to the bride and the groom? In verse one we see that you can use all kinds of love talk, speak in eloquent words, impress each other with your wit, but if there is not *love*, all your words are nothing but noise. From verse two we might infer that you may have read all the books on love, spent many hours at college studying psychology, know all the mysteries of marriage, plan all you can plan for a happy home, but if there is not *love*, your marriage is nothing. From verse three we should learn that you can sacrifice for each other, buy all sorts of gifts, work your hands to the bone, but if there is not *love,* you have not gained a thing. This *love* of which St. Paul speaks is that redemptive, sacrificial love in Christ that prompted God to save you from all sin and death. When you honestly have this *love,* then your marriage can be promised a beautiful future. It is this selfless love that occurs in marriage. And in this selfless love, God places sex.

Read Ephesians 5:21–33. This is another favorite wedding text for Christian couples. Let us study and understand what Paul is saying.

Frequently, this passage is misunderstood. Oftentimes we imagine this relationship to look like this:

| | | |
|---|---|---|
| ***Christ*** | ——— | ***Husband*** |
| ***Church*** | | ***Wife*** |

We imagine the husband is in a greater position than the wife and the wife dutifully supports him, unnoticed. This is not true. In fact, the picture looks quite the opposite. Just as Christ is proud of His bride the Church, He presents her pure before the world. Similarly, the husband presents his wife pure and precious before the world.

| | | |
|---|---|---|
| ***Church*** | ——— | ***Wife*** |
| ***Christ*** | | ***Husband*** |

In this way, great honor, not inferiority, is given to the wife.

As the husband lovingly presents his wife to the world, so also does the wife support and comfort her husband out of love.

Read Ephesians 5:21–33 again. Paul is speaking of the beautiful relationships in God's plan: a marriage should reflect the selfless love of Christ. As Christ sacrifices Himself for us, so will a man's love be sacrificial for a woman. In this way, the responsibility is upon the man. He is to present her "without stain" (Ephesians 5:27). A woman receives the love of a man as we receive the love and sacrifices of Christ. With this sort of sacrificial, pure love, any woman is willing to obey a man who is so willing to sacrifice himself for her protection. If a man can love a woman the way Christ loves His church, he will have no trouble in gaining her full respect and esteem.

In this way, young men present your girlfriends and the women in your life as prized children of God, protecting the purity, not taking it from them. And Christian women, care and support the Christian men in your life, encouraging them in Christ. Reflect on Paul's picture of marriage. Do you think it is workable?

## "You shall not steal"

We are in an age that is crazy about "things." Everybody is judged by the number of things they possess. We hear the philosophy of our generation labeled with such words as "materialism" and "secularism." These words say that the material and worldly things in life are what really matter. They say that life centers around what a person owns. We simply "have to have" certain clothes, a certain type of car, certain electronics and entertainment. All of this makes money the big factor. We must have money. Young people feel that money is one of the most important factors for their ultimate success and happiness in life.

St. Paul wrote, "The love of money is the root of all evil." There is divine truth in this. Most of our human problems are conflicts in the realm of economics. We can see this between nations. We can see this in our communities. We can see this between a husband and wife. The love of money or greed has ruined more relationships between people and has twisted the lives of more men and women than probably any other single factor.

The Seventh Commandment, therefore, is very relevant to humanity. It speaks about more than simply robbing a bank or stealing pencils from the office. The Seventh Commandment shows us how deeply rooted our old sinful nature is as we see our sinful greed. This commandment shows the Christian the joy of helping those less financially fortunate because he or she has known the redemption of God in Jesus Christ, our Savior. Jesus has given us a new relationship with God. This means that our money and all that we have are not our possessions, but gifts from God. In this relationship with God, we are able to see how little the material possessions of this world compare with God's great gift of heaven.

Therefore, the young Christian does not work for money. He or she works for God. The job or profession becomes a way of serving God with the talents God has given him or her. No job, profession, or vocation must ever be chosen because the pay is good or the money is easy. The Christian chooses a vocation in the light of the Gospel of Jesus Christ. This means that the individual will perform his or her daily work not for the sake of money or the reputation it will bring, but rather because it gives the opportunity and the joy of serving God as a faithful "child." And serving God means serving our neighbors by contributing to their temporal and eternal welfare.

Our age needs young men and women redeemed by God who can reveal the life of Jesus Christ in the area of economic existence. Here is one of the devil's strongest holds on humanity. You can be God's answer to the frightening materialism and secularism of our day.

## Reflections

Study the following references: Matthew 24:42–51; Luke 19:11–26; 1 Corinthians 4:2; 1 Peter 4:10. On some pages in the New Testament we are called "stewards." Sometimes this is translated "servant." We talk a lot about stewardship today, but this does not mean we always know what we are talking about. Too often we think of the word *money* when we think of stewardship. This is a wrong thought. Study your references, and see what God thinks. First, God thinks that a steward is one no longer his or her own. Stewards in the Bible were not lords or masters, though they were not slaves either. They handled a lot of real estate, but it wasn't their own. They handled a great deal of cash, but they were not free to do with it as they chose. They took care of their master's business as a high ranking servant. This was a high position for a servant. Even still, everything, including themselves, belonged to their "lord" or master. God says you are His stewards. Everything you have or are belongs to Him and must be used for Him. Secondly, God thinks that you will manage everything on His behalf. You will use all your gifts for His cause. Thirdly, God knows that if you believe in the Lord Jesus Christ, you will be this kind of steward.

→

Stewardship is what happens to a person's life when Jesus gets hold of him or her. This is what God makes clear in His Word. What do you think?

Read Amos 4:1–3 and 8:1–6. This prophet of God thunders against the economic and social injustice of his day. His words are hard and sharp. He called certain women the "cows of Bashan." Speaking to our generation, Amos says they demand that their husbands bring home more money in their paychecks so that they can have more parties, more clothes and a better house. And they don't care how their husbands get that money. In 8:1–6 we see the vision of the basket of summer fruit. This vision says that Israel is "ripe" for judgment. They are becoming more and more rotten as the days go by. How can Amos say this? Read 8:4–6 again. It is the old, old picture of the big man beating out the little man; of dishonesty in business; of scheming for power; of living your life for your own success in this world and not caring about the next person. No nation that performs such iniquity will escape the judgment of God. This includes our nation too. Just think what Amos could say today—to us. Give this serious thought.

## "You shall not give false testimony against your neighbor"

Few things are as damaging to the Christian church as the behind-the-back whispering, the gossiping tongue, the slander one person does to another. Here Satan has his most vicious weapon. It breaks up what God puts together and destroys what God has created. If one commandment can be singled out as the least heeded by Christians in their holy fellowship, it is the Eighth Commandment.

It is hard to undo a lie. Take a pillow filled with feathers and tear it apart and scatter those feathers to the wind. Then say to your friend, "Go, pick up all those feathers." Your friend will answer, "This is impossible. I can get most of them, but certainly not all." Once a lie is out, there is no way to correct every bit of it. When you slander the name of another in any manner or form, no matter what you do to retract and undo your slander, you will never gather in all the evil of your untruth.

The Eighth Commandment directs the Christian beyond God's order not to tell a lie. It shows the person that he or she must speak the truth. As followers of our Lord Jesus Christ, whom we confess as the Truth, we must always confess truth if we are to confess Him. If you know something to be true, but keep silent, you deny your Lord. If you know something to be false, but do not have the courage to speak against it, you become a Peter and deny that you know the truth.

Your Christian life, which is imbedded in your Lord Jesus Christ, must be a witness for the truth. This is more than just a concern for the truth. Everybody has that to some extent. It is the willingness to speak the truth, even if it means to be crucified for the truth. To speak truth may mean that your popularity, your position, your material advancement, your family's safety might be at stake. In times like these you must look up at the cross and see what lies did to the Truth. This is why Jesus said to you, "Take up [your] *cross* and follow Me" (Matthew 16:24).

Yet the cross and the open tomb speak of the victory of Christ over Satan, of the Truth over the father of lies. In the realm of truth

there is the Way and there is the Life. You have little choice, dear follower of Jesus. In our world of lies, the truth must be proclaimed
and must not be hidden. In every circumstance of men it must be
spoken. And it is up to you to speak it.

## Reflections

Read John 8. Here is one of Jesus' brilliant discourses with
the Jews concerning the matter of truth. All truth is bound
up in Jesus (see John 14:6). In Jesus Christ a man is introduced to what truth really is. This truth makes a man free
(see verses 34–36). Verses 42–47 give Jesus' penetrating
judgment upon the lie and upon people who speak lies. He
does not hide His feelings. As you reflect upon this chapter,
give thought to the world in which you live. Truly it belongs
to the "lie." The "lie" is seen in our advertising, in the cor-
ruption in our cities, in powerful people in powerful places,
and in the little people in little places. It is all around us.
Those who know the truth will be free from sin (verse 32);
those who do not know the truth will be slaves to sin (verses 34–35). The former will receive eternal life in heaven; the
latter, eternal condemnation in hell.

Read James 3:1–12. A wise man once was asked by a king
what part of the human body can do the most good and
also do the most harm. The wise man answered the king and
said, "The tongue." You probably know this all too well from
experience. Listen to what James says here, and use your
tongue as God would want you to. Here is a little rule that

→

may help you speak the truth and not fall victim to speaking lies and slander. When you speak about somebody, make sure that what you are saying is true, not just half true. Look at your motivation—be sure you can speak it in the concern and love of Jesus Christ for the good of that person. And finally, ask yourself whether it is necessary that you say it at all.

## "You shall not covet . . ."

The saying goes that the grass is greener on the other side of the fence. This was Adam and Eve's problem. Satan painted a picture of greener pastures than what they were enjoying. In seeking the greener pastures, Adam and Eve revolted against God.

It has been this way ever since. People have always sought to obtain things to satisfy themselves. They have always wanted to be "as gods." They have always wanted to have certain things they thought they had coming to them. So people have learned to covet that which belongs to their "neighbor."

Covetousness comes quite naturally to us. We covet what the next person has. We covet her good looks and personality. We desire to have his car or clothes. We look with jealous eyes at the person who always gets the best grades (without studying). Then Satan speaks to us and says, "If only you had what he has!" "If you only were as good as her!"

But to covet is a far more subtle temptation than just the obvious passion to obtain what the other person has. It manifests itself in many kinds of "virtues." We say, "We must defend our rights," only to cover up our greedy hearts. We make a virtue out of our national interests, even when it means oppressing others to boost our economy. We make a virtue out of profit making, holding up this as success, even if this means that the little people get hurt in business. We have almost made a god out of advertising. It tells us daily what we need, want, and must have. It tells a family to buy the latest model because the one of last year belongs to the middle ages, even when so many families cannot afford to buy. And advertisers have set up young people as their special targets, since they put real pressure on their families.

In this age where covetousness is nurtured all about us, God's command speaks and says, "Do not covet!" We dare not cover up our coveting with all sorts of gods and virtues either. Faith in our Lord Jesus Christ demands that we be separated from this world even though He wants us to live in it. He wants us to live in it as lights and as salt. It is only the life that you have in the Lord Jesus that can take your eyes off what other people have and place it upon what other people need. In Jesus all coveting disappears, and you learn to minister and no longer want to be ministered to.

## Reflections

Read Luke 12:13–31. Covetousness gives a person two things: poor perspective and worry. Jesus addresses perspective in verses 13–21 and worry in verses 22–31. The man in Jesus' parable had poor perspective on life. He could not see beyond himself. He could not see beyond this world. He equated his life with the amount of goods he could accumulate for himself. He is imitated by so many couples today who feel that a home is a home when it is filled with things. So they work themselves to the bone, not having any children till the right time, so that they may have their house, their two cars, their furniture, their wall-to-wall carpeting. They think they know what life is all about, but they can't see beyond themselves. They can't see beyond this world into the new world of Jesus Christ. In verses 22–31 Jesus deals with anxiety and worry. No nation takes more pills to remove worry and tension than ours. The reason is in verse 30. America seeks after "things." In this world of "things," seek after the kingdom of God.

Read Luke 15:11–24. This familiar story of the prodigal son is but one of the lost stories in Luke 15. This chapter is often called the "Lost Chapter," because it contains parables of the "lost sheep," "the lost coin," and "the lost boy." Actually all three parables were spoken to reveal the love God has for the sinner; therefore, the emphasis is on God, not upon humans. Yet you can see humanity is well described in this last parable as the sin of covetousness is most apparent. Study the results of a covetous heart as you read through this parable:

| 12 | self-will |
| 13 | selfishness |
| 13 | separation |
| 13 | sensuality |
| 14 | spiritual destitution |
| 15 | self-abasement |
| 16 | starvation |

→

These seven downward steps resulted from a young boy's covetous heart. Jesus teaches all youth a real lesson here. Look at yourself and see if this is not true in your own life.

Reflections on

# The
# LoRd's Prayer

## "Our Father who art in heaven"

Prayer is the sacred privilege of the children of God. It is a heavenly gift. In prayer you ask to be heard by the almighty God. Nothing else will content you. This is what we do in prayer—we ask in the name of His Son who intercedes for us. We ask to be listened to. We petition the Creator of all things to give ear to and to grant our requests.

In this very beautiful prayer taught us by Christ, we call God "Father." Yet no man can call God "Father" unless God adopts him or her into His holy family. All too frequently you hear people call God "Father" as though it were their choice to create the family of heaven. God permits only His children to call Him "Father." Who are His children? His children are those whom He recognizes in His Son, Jesus Christ, because they believe in Him. When you received the Lord Jesus into your heart, God received you into His family. Thus you—not just anybody—have been given privilege of calling Him "Father" whenever you pray.

How easy God wants it to be for us to talk to Him! It is so important for both the redeemed and the Redeemer, the creature and the Creator, the sanctified and the Sanctifier, to have and use a medium of communication. God knows this. He wants us to know it too. He talks to you in His Word. You talk to Him in prayer. Here is the reality of the atonement in Jesus Christ's redeeming death. Atonement, sometimes written as "At-one-ment," means we can walk and talk with God as a child does with his father. Never do we degrade this privilege as a form of divine-human chumminess; it is too sacred and awesome for such an idea as this. But there is certainly no fear in this relationship. There is only room for growth in understanding God Himself.

What ungrateful children we would be if we did I not take seriously this heavenly gift and open it daily and use it lovingly. God is waiting this very moment for you to pray to Him. Let's begin: "Our Father, who art in heaven. . . ."

# Reflections

Read John 15:1–11. The "Vine Chapter" tells us that we are the children of God only as we abide in Him and He in us. This abiding presence of God the Father in and with His children is the guarantee that He will forever abide in and with them in heaven. Here we see the importance of prayer and the goal of prayer. As you reflect on these words of our Lord, keep the following thoughts in mind: Why must I abide in Christ? What is the purpose of abiding in Christ? What is the joy of abiding in Christ? The answer to these inquiries should be: Abiding in Christ!

## Abiding in Christ —

| is ... | because | verse |
|---|---|---|
| Absolutely necessary | only Christ can do good works and without Him one can do nothing | 5–6 |
| Communion with God | the prayers of one who abides in Jesus are heard and answered | 7 |
| For a purpose | God may be glorified by this testimony of His disciples | 8 |

Read Romans 8:31–39. This is a wonderful passage to take to heart. What has this to do with prayer? Everything! Once the spirit of this portion of God's Word touches your heart, you will find a new life in prayer. Look at verse 32. Where else in all of Scripture is there a promise greater than this? It gives us assurance that our prayers are heard and answered. It gives us the confidence needed to pray. It gives us the direction in the words "with Him." It speaks of Jesus interceding for us right now (verse 34). Truly, we are more than conquerors (verse 37). People who believe this cannot help but pray—pray with power, faith, and thanksgiving.

## "Hallowed be Thy name"

You cannot meditate on this first petition very long without seeing the apparent relationship with the Second Commandment. Both deal with the holy name of God. The one is set at the beginning of the Lord's Prayer, the other at the beginning of the commandments. It is obvious that God takes His name seriously and that He expects man to take it seriously too. In the commandments He warns that no one will be held guiltless who takes His name in vain. In this model prayer He teaches how His name may be hallowed by all those who believe in the saving name of His Son.

You cannot comprehend the thoughts of God here unless you first realize the blasphemy His holy name suffered in the fall of man. Before this part of His creation fell into its rebellious state, everything in the cosmos revealed the holiness of the name of God. There was harmony not only in a physical sense but also in a spiritual sense that transcends our highest thoughts. Since the fall, humankind has been able to do everything but make God's name holy on earth. By word, thought, and actions, humans have blasphemed it. If you feel that this is an exaggerated statement, you only have to look closely at the agonizing and cruel cross that clearly shows us the results of such blasphemy.

Yet it is because of this cross that *you* have been reconciled into the family of God again. Therefore you are the one Jesus teaches to pray, "Hallowed be Thy name." Only believers can pray this. Why? Because only they will be actively interested in the petition they are praying. For example, when you say to your busy mother, "Mom, I'd like the house to be spotless for my friends," you can't say this with sincerity as you walk out the door to hang out with your friends. If this statement comes from the heart, you will help scrub the floors, move the furniture, dust, and clean.

In this first petition you are saying, "Heavenly Father, since You have made me Your child in the Lord Jesus, I'd like to see the holiness and goodness of Your name felt upon this earth." You can't mean this and walk out on God. You can only pray this and then reflect God's goodness to everybody around you. This is what Jesus meant when He said *you* must be a salty salt. Your desire is to flavor your relationships with the goodness and holiness connected with the name of your Lord. A little girl commented on this, saying that one of the qualities of salt is that it makes you thirsty. Have you made anyone thirsty for the Lord Jesus? Listen to Him as He teaches you to pray, "Hallowed be Thy name."

# Reflections

Open your Bible and see how Jesus hallowed the name of His Father. On two occasions of Jesus' ministry God made the statement, "This is My beloved Son, in whom I am well pleased." The first time was at the beginning of Jesus' ministry as Jesus set out to reveal who He was (see Matthew 3:17). The second time was at His transfiguration as Jesus set out to perform the task His Father planned (see Matthew 17:5). No wonder the Father was delighted in Jesus, for in Him the Father found a man who did everything as perfectly on earth as it is done in heaven. In everything that Jesus did or said, God's name was hallowed among men. It was never blasphemed, but always glorified. Thus Jesus prays this first petition in His own words, "Father, glorify Your name" (John 12:28). The Father answers Jesus' prayer by saying that His name has been and will be glorified. How? Read the surrounding verses, John 12:23–33. Jesus is thinking of His coming crucifixion for the sins of men. In this sacrificial act of redemption God's name was glorified. On the cross His name was hallowed as in no other way on this earth. With St. Paul, you can find glory in the cross of Christ and receive the power to hallow the name of God as did our Lord.

Think on what Jesus is saying in the words, "And I will do whatever you ask in My name, so that the Son may bring glory to the Father" (John 14:13). We hallow God's name by using prayer. When we pray in the name of our Lord, God is glorified. This passage says two things to us. First, it speaks of praying in the name of the Lord Jesus. There is no other name by which humanity has a reconciled relationship with God. Therefore in His name we speak to God, knowing we shall be heard. But it also means that we pray according to His purpose. For example, when a lawyer has the power of attorney, it means that he can speak and act for his client. The attorney does things in the name of his client and for the ultimate good of his client. If the attorney no longer carries out the will of the person who hired him, he is relieved of his power of attorney. In a sense this is what is meant here in this passage. Jesus has given us the power of attorney. As we perform His will, our prayer is answered. And by praying and acting in His name, God Himself is glorified. Second, this encourages us to pray. People of prayer have always been people who have hallowed the name of God on earth. It takes people of prayer to act in that name. Therefore, to hallow the name of God, "call upon it—pray— praise—give thanks."

### "Thy kingdom come"

Every time you pray this petition, you recognize that there are two kingdoms. There is the kingdom of God and the kingdom not of God. There is a realm where God is the Ruler and one where Satan rules with the powers of sin and death. These two kingdoms are opposites at every point; therefore, conflict and warfare are inevitable when they meet.

Every time you pray this petition you are asking God to invade and conquer the kingdom of Satan. God's great invasion and conquest came in the person and in the work of His Son. Christ's first coming—His incarnation, His life, His death, His resurrection—all tell the story of that great invasion and conquest. But Christ has not yet eternally chained Satan. Satan, though conquered by Christ, is still permitted to prowl about as a roaring lion. Constantly there is conflict. Jesus speaks of love—Satan of hate. Satan says, "Hit back;" Jesus says, "Turn the other cheek." Jesus says "Bless," where Satan cries "Curse." Jesus is Truth and Life; Satan is the Lie and Death.

God's invasion and conquest climaxed on a battleground called Calvary. The strange thing about this battle was that both used the same weapon—a cross. Satan led sinful men to nail Christ to the cross, but in the process of being nailed to this cross, Christ took all of man's sin upon Himself. Christ did this so that He might draw all men back to God again and to salvation.

You cannot pray the words "Thy kingdom come" unless you are identified with God's kingdom. You cannot say that you want God's rule to come into this world unless His rule is first set up in your heart. This means that you have no other master but God and His Son Jesus Christ. You desire to serve no one in your life but Him. Many want to call Jesus "Savior," because they want to be saved from hell. But few want to call Jesus "Lord," because they want to have life their own way.

Jesus wants and needs young men and women to pray this petition. In a world where so many are in Satan's power, Jesus wants people like you who are sold on His kingdom. This petition separates the true Christian from the untrue, for you are inviting conflict and a hard struggle. So look all about you at the evil foe, and strap on the Gospel armor and ready yourself for real battle. Then say, "Lord, now let Thy kingdom come!"

# Reflections

Read Luke 11:14–23. Compare this narrative with Romans 5:17–21. Jesus clearly sets up Satan's kingdom in contrast with that of God. His power over Satan's rule (Luke 11:20) demonstrates the invasion of the kingdom of God. No man has been able to overcome Satan and overthrow his rule, for no man has overcome death, sin, and hell. But Jesus Christ is the stronger One (Luke 11:22), for He has overcome sin, death, and hell. This is what Paul is thinking of in his Letter to the Romans, in chapter 5:17–21. Each verse tells of the conflict between the two realms. But what is more important, Paul shows how in the Lord Jesus Christ we now have the rule of God's grace for a life of righteousness. In this truth lies the heart of our Christian faith and the purpose of the Christian church.

Read the thirteenth chapter of Matthew. The entire chapter deals with parables concerning the kingdom of heaven. Each parable of Jesus can give you rich insight into the meaning of the kingdom of heaven. As you read, reflect on the following:

| The parable | What it shows about the kingdom |
| --- | --- |
| —The Sower | As God's Word is received, so is its victory |
| —The Weeds | The inevitability of conflict |
| —The Mustard Seed | The promised growth |
| —The Yeast | Its universal influence |
| —The Hidden Treasure | The joy in finding it |
| —The Pearl | Its immeasurable worth |
| —The Net | It demands a final judgment |

## "Thy will be done on earth as it is in heaven"

Prayer is a spiritual process of getting in gear with the mind of God. It is a spiritual exercise to align the believer's will with the will of God. It is a means of getting in sync with the thinking of God.

A well-known Bible commentator gave this illustration on prayer. Once there was a man who purchased a very expensive violin and the sheet music of many famous symphonies. The man had one of the most expensive plasma televisions with the best surround sound capabilities. He always wanted to play with big orchestras, but never could. His idea was to play his violin at home by following his music of the symphony and playing with the orchestra as it was played on public television. He would check the program listing to find out which songs would be played. Then he turned on the TV program with his music in front of him and play. At first he missed beats and lost his place and made his violin sound like fingernails on the chalkboard. But in time, he mastered the art of it and managed to play along rather easily with the great orchestras. Now if this man would refuse to tune his violin, or if he decided to play Brahm's First while the television station had scheduled Haydn's Surprise Symphony, there would be no harmonious music. There would be jagged, annoying discords. Or if this man shut off his television because he didn't like the selection, this would in no way stop the station's music from flying over the airwaves.

The comparison is clear. You pray, "Thy will be done on earth as it is in heaven." In fact, you can be assured that God's will is being carried out on earth according to His eternal purpose. But you are praying that you can become part of His will, or that His will can become your will. Thus you seek the harmony of your will to the Father's and the alignment of your life with His Son's. Prayer is definitely a spiritual art that few know, thus few have mastered. Your natural will does not want to play the same piece that God is playing in His heavenly orchestra. But in prayer, seeking prayer, listening prayer, earnest prayer, your ear will become attuned to heaven's pitch, and your life will become more in harmony with your heavenly Father's will.

Never will you want to turn God off, as though going your own way could ever stop the great design of God. But you pray that you can become a real part of His holy will, that through you a part of God's grand purpose might find fulfillment.

## Reflections

Read Mark 9:14–29. The emphasis that Jesus wants to make is in verse 29. What does Jesus mean, "This kind can come out only by prayer"? The disciples were unable to cast out the demon in this boy (verse 18), even though they had this power and used it (see 6:7–13, especially verse 13). They had the power, but they lost it! Jesus' words in 9:29 give us the answer to why the disciples were unable to cast out the demons (verses 27–28). Jesus says that only by prayer can a Christian keep the good gifts God has given him. The disciples' failure lay in the failure to give time and perseverance to prayer. They got out of gear with the power and the will of God. Many young people are confirmed in the church each year. Yet as they grow up in their teens, they no longer come to worship. They lose all interest in the Word of God,

➔

and become lost to the church. Why? Because that which was given to them at their confirmation was lost. It was lost because they failed to spend time in prayer, the study of God's Word, and participating in Holy Communion.

Read the fourth chapter of Jonah. Here Jonah confesses that he was not in gear with the will of God. He was not sympathetic to the grace of God. In chapters one and two Jonah tells how he tried to run away, but how God appointed a great fish to swallow him up, and how God finally saved him from inevitable death. In chapters three and four, Jonah tells how he now responds to God's command (3:1–3) by going to Nineveh and preaching God's message. In chapter four Jonah confesses how disappointed and bitter he was that Nineveh repented and that they did not receive their deserved judgment from God (verses 1–3). Jonah had experienced God's grace, being saved from the belly of the fish. Jonah was willing to preach God's grace to a million people who had many grievous sins upon their heads. But Jonah was unwilling to love those people with the same love that God did. Jonah was unwilling to become involved in God's grace toward others. Jonah has written this confession for you. You desire God's grace for yourself. You don't care if God wants to love *all* people (for God is Love), but you don't like to always become involved in this grace of God. You don't want to get into gear with the will of your heavenly Father. You say, "If God wants to love that person I don't like, that is His business. But why involve me with His kind of love?" Don't you see? You commit Jonah's sin over and over again in your reaction to diversity problems, to the mission call of the church, to your youth group. Here is reason for real prayer, much prayer. Get in gear with the holy will of God; become

## "Give us this day our daily bread"

Many times we are not happy with the clothes we have. We want new and better clothes. Perhaps we have been irritated that mom drives such an out-of-date car or that the house is so small. Like so many young people, we often become so concerned about our dress, the kind of car we drive, the security promised by a specific vocation, the money we can earn, that we have not learned the joy of true living.

Jesus is very concerned that we learn the joy of true living. Happy living begins in enjoying what God has already given to us. You probably can think of someone you know who is happy though he or she has little material wealth and very limited social security. Such a person has caught the secret of Jesus' words, "Give us this day our daily bread."

In the fourth petition of the Lord's Prayer you learn to pray for the essentials in life. Jesus speaks of bread. Bread represents the common essentials of life. We do not need cake for daily nutrition, but we do need bread. We do not need the latest styles in dress, but we do need clothes. We do not need a five-bedroom, five-bath mansion, but we do need a home. In this petition we must forget what we would like or what is not essential for true living, and think solely upon the essentials.

Jesus teaches us to say "daily bread" too. This is difficult to say. We are taught today by the world not to think of just today but of our future security. We are in a nation that is asking for a security system from the cradle to the grave. We are conditioned to select our career on the amount of security a job or profession can offer. In this atmosphere Jesus says we must learn to live day by day with God. We must learn to trust His unconditional guarantee that He will provide for those who do His will as their needs require each day.

The story goes that the blue jay was so concerned about his dress at creation that he never learned how to sing. When you can rejoice each day over the essential things for true living, then will you learn the secret for confident living. This is what you must feel when you pray, "Give us this day our daily bread." Do not ask for more, and do not expect less. Let Jesus teach you true happiness through this petition. Learn from Him that you must go through each day looking up, not just looking down.

# Reflections

Read the sixteenth chapter of Exodus. This familiar Old Testament story gives us great insight into God's provisions for us, His children. Bread and meat are essentials to a daily diet. God provided for the Israelites, but only with the food necessary for daily sustenance. No more, but no less. Because God provided only enough for their *daily* need, the Israelites were not to store food away for the next day (verses 19–20). Such an idea was an insult to God, saying that He was not to be trusted for daily bread (verse 21). God fulfilled His promise to take care of the Israelites with

→

manna and quail. In verses 32–34, the manna becomes one of the articles of the Ark of the Covenant to be a witness to God's daily provision for His own. Since they ate manna for forty years, God's promise proved true. We ask for daily bread because we know that God each day will give us what we need for this body and life.

Think about the following three passages in the light of the fourth petition: Hebrews 11:13–16; 13:14, and 1 Peter 2:11. Every one speaks of the Christian as a stranger and pilgrim on earth. Our hope is not in the earth or in the things of earth. It is in the new heaven and the new earth where Jesus Christ is All in all. Therefore Jesus teaches us to say "daily bread," lest we get lost in matters of this life and forget that we belong to the world yet to come.

## "And forgive us our trespasses as we forgive those who trespass against us"

If any man truly grasps the full meaning of the forgiveness of sins in Jesus Christ, he understands the entire Scripture. The forgiveness of sins is the common denominator for every theological equation. Yet nothing is harder to do than to forgive someone's sin against you. The forgiveness of sins is the most difficult activity for anybody to perform. Was it hard for God, too?

Look again at the cross of your Lord, nailed to the accursed tree by the sins of men, and you will begin to understand how hard it was for God to forgive humans their iniquity. Forgiveness comes hard because it hurts, true, but this is not all. Forgiveness comes hard because it demands that you sacrificially give yourself in part or in whole to the one who sinned against you. This takes trust as you not only forgive the sinner, but *forget* the sin done against you. It is this way because God gives us His "All" in order truly to forgive us our sins. Forgiven, they are "as far as the east is from the west" (Psalm 103:12) from God's mind.

The cross is a wonderful symbol of forgiveness. When you forgive somebody who has hurt you with a slandering tongue, you crucify any bitterness that you have toward that person. When you crucify that bitterness, it will become dead to you. You will be cleansed in the very process of your forgiving. To forgive another from the heart often hurts, because it is in opposition to our sinful nature. Forgiveness is difficult.

The power of the fifth petition lies in the forgiveness that you have experienced through the redeeming work of Jesus Christ. Through this forgiving act God brought you into His family. By this same activity in His Son, God will give to you the strength to forgive others, especially those who you find it very hard to forgive and those loveless acts that you find harder to forget.

Forgiving others is one of the more difficult things God asks you to do. But He says that you must do this because you are part of His family. You are part of His family because He has forgiven you. Your forgiveness depends entirely on Christ's atonement. You *cannot earn* forgiveness by forgiving others, but you *forfeit and lose* your forgiveness by refusing to forgive others.

# Reflections

Read Isaiah 1:1–18. There is probably no place in Scripture where the iniquity of mankind is so clearly analyzed and so definitely shown to be inexcusable. At the same time no section of Scripture gives a better picture of God's forgiveness. Isaiah begins by calling on the heavens and the earth, for they have been witnesses over the centuries to God's unfailing grace and goodness. With these witnesses listening and watching, Isaiah gives more credit to the ox and the donkey, which know whose they are and who takes care of them, than he can give to the Israelites. His searing condemnation can be compared to Paul's in Romans 3:10–20. In verse 18, Isaiah speaks for the Lord, saying, "Come now, and let us reason together." In the original Hebrew, he is saying that all the condemned people should come before the Lord and see how their sins balance out in the scales of God's justice. Naturally you expect convinced damnation will follow. But into this scene of justice comes God's forgiving grace, "Though your sins be as scarlet, they shall be as white as snow. . . ." No clearer picture can show how God forgives the sinner. There is nothing in the sinner that makes God want to forgive him. Yet God's forgiveness is radical and complete. It places the condemned sinner in a new and exciting relationship with God and God in a fresh and blessed relationship with the sinner.

Read Matthew 18:21–35. To forgive means to love. If you say, "I'll forgive you, but I won't forget what you said," your forgiveness is not real because you still are failing to love. The parable needs little explanation. The point is clearly summarized by our Lord in verse 35. The next time you find it hard to forgive somebody who has done something against you, put yourself in the place of the offender and put God in your place. See how it feels not to be forgiven fully, completely, and lovingly. Then look again at your offender, and realize how much he or she needs your forgiveness and how much you need to forgive.

## "And lead us not into temptation"

Humans like the idea of being led into temptation. People like to be led into sin, especially if no one will catch them. Temptation looks very thrilling, and we wish that God would turn His back for a moment. We think that if we can't experience this or that thrill, God will cheat us of really living. This is one of Satan's cleverly invented lies.

Satan whispers the same line to you as he did to Adam and Eve. He says, God hasn't told you the whole truth. God is holding out on you. God can't help that He is so holy. Besides, He will forgive you this once. So you let yourself be led into temptation. You hang out with the wrong crowd. You get ready for a passionate night of making-out with your date. You try a hit of a drug. After all, how do you know what sin is like unless you try it? Let's face it—you like to be led into temptation.

But in the sixth petition you pray, "Lord, lead me not into temptation." Never think for one moment that God would ever lead you into temptation. The Lord doesn't lead you there. Satan does. What you are praying is this: "Lord, I like to be led into temptation, and Satan enjoys leading me there. But I want You to be my Leader. I want You to lead me away from temptation. I want You to lead me on Your path of goodness. Lord, if I pray about it and seem repentant, then it will be okay to do it. Right?"

Why do you like to be seduced by Satan? Why do you like to be led into sin? This very question proves Scripture's truth when it says you were born a sinner. You were born with the will to like what God doesn't like. You were born fighting against God's goodness, truth, and love. But God has redeemed you in His Son Jesus Christ to lead you away from all iniquity and sin and temptation to the new life of His kingdom. God knows that if He doesn't, you will let Satan dominate you, enslave you, and take you to hell.

Because of this, you will want to pray from the heart, "Lord, don't let Satan lead me into temptation. Lead me, O Lord, in Your ways. For Your ways are life—real life!" Satan will never let you pray this petition easily. He will try to make you pray it with doubts. All he wants or needs is a foothold in the door of your heart. But this is why our Lord Jesus has taught us to pray this petition in the model prayer. He, too, was tempted. He knows what it is all about. He also overcame Satan and all temptation. In Jesus you can too.

# Reflections

Study the following passages: 1 Corinthians 6:18; 10:14; 1 Timothy 6:11; 2 Timothy 2:22. The one word that Paul uses in each one of these exhortations is "flee." The one way not to be led into temptation is to flee from it. In fact, if you deliberately stand in the path of temptation, you are sinning, even though the temptation itself fails. This advice of Paul is directed especially to young people. See 2 Timothy 2:22, where Paul specifically says "youthful lusts." The devil is tricky, telling us that we can handle ourselves in this or that situation. Just because you know someone who has had sex and hasn't gotten pregnant or tried drugs and isn't an addict, doesn't mean you should try it. Satan deceives us by telling us false messages. Oftentimes we wake up to the truth only to recognize Satan's control over our lives. You can't lean against a freshly painted wall and not walk away unmarked. You can't play with sex without misusing your body, without hurting yourself and the other emotionally. You can't hang around the wrong crowd and not come out bad. You can't cheat "this once" and not have it affect your ethical outlook later in life. So St. Paul says in all these passages, "Flee!" Why flee? Why not fight? Because you can't fight some of these. Take sex, for example. It is a natural drive. But to push the line is asking for temptation and lust to take control. St. Paul understood young people. He says, "Flee." Get out of there. Better yet, don't get yourself into a situation that is ready for sin.

Think about Paul's words in Philippians 4:4–8. Verse 8 discusses how to control our thoughts. If you honestly do not wish to be led into temptation, then you have to see that you are led into the right paths. How? Paul's few words tell you. Select those things that are true and pure and lovely. This warning applies to friends, television, movies, magazines, and so on. If you read or watch trash you are setting yourself to be tempted in trashy things. What you read and see controls what you think. Take Paul's advice seriously. You can't "rejoice in the Lord" and rejoice in a movie that the

→

Lord would despise. Guard the control of your thoughts. It is the best way not to be led into temptation.

### "But deliver us from evil"

There is a somber tone to this last petition. In a sense it is a summary of the Lord's Prayer. It recognizes the two great truths of God's Word: first, that deliverance belongs to the Lord and second, that the world in which we live is very evil. It makes us look about us and inside of us, but it also makes us look up. It is prayed with confidence, yet with sober reflection.

Deliverance belongs to the Lord, writes the psalmist. Jonah cried this out from the fish's belly. In the final analysis, it is God who delivers. It is God who saves. Evil is not a power that we can overcome by ourselves. Evil is a power from which we must be delivered. Jesus Christ has delivered us from the power of sin and death. As a result of Christ's action, we can be delivered from all evil.

Evil is all about us. Nations are at war and terrorism kills the innocent. Business is a game of moral decay as individuals and corporations race to have the most money. Society weaves a web of lies that sex is a casual event between any two people who want it.

The daily news program tells of a family of six who were killed in a head-on collision; sixty who died in a plane crash; a wife murdered by her husband; millions starving to death; injustice; teenage delinquency; lying and stealing. You can't turn on television without saying to yourself, "Lord, deliver us from all this evil."

Then you begin to think about your future. What kind of future is there in a world like this? What is all this talk about security when evil drowns out every kind of social protection? This is why Jesus taught you to pray, "Deliver us from evil." In this petition you have the confidence, strength, and courage to face both the present and the future.

God will deliver you from all evil. Nothing can ever separate His deliverance from your hour of need. Jesus said, "I have overcome the world!" His cross and open tomb prove this. Yes, there is evil; much evil. But the Lord Jesus will deliver you from all evil; that is why to Him and the Father and the Spirit is the kingdom and the power and the glory forever.

# Reflections

Read Ephesians 6:10–20. Paul was in prison when he wrote this letter. What do you think gave him the idea for his description of the Christian's armor? Carefully note each piece of fighting equipment Paul mentions that you will need to fight the evil one. Write it down on the first list. Place its purpose in the second, and what would happen if you leave it off on the third. Remember Paul's words in verse 12. Your battle is not only with your own sinful flesh, but also with the evil all around you. God can, and does, equip you!

→

| Piece of armor | Purpose | Result if not put on |
|---|---|---|
| 1. | | |
| 2. | | |
| 3. | | |
| 4. | | |
| 5. | | |
| 6. | | |

Read Revelation 19:1–16. This chapter of St. John has the theme of victory. It says we are more than conquerors in Jesus Christ. Verses 1–8 are a song of praise to God, who has delivered His own from all evil. Evil may have looked as if it won the day, but in the end all will see that evil and Satan will be overthrown. God promises inevitable victory. Young people, led by the Rider on the white horse (verse 11), are still an army conquering and to conquer. Here is the march of progress of the Gospel of Jesus Christ. Salvation is God's work. God will deliver. Therefore to Him belongs the kingdom, the power, and the glory (verse 1).